THE SPENDING WINDOW

How Intermittent Spending Can Improve Your Finances

Daniel J. Wendol, CFP®
Angelo R. DeRosalia, MD

AUTHOR'S NOTE

This book is a collaboration between two friends but was ultimately written in the voice of only one. This was done to allow the text to be more conversational, plus, Dan had more experience with sharing financial topics due to his day to day profession.

How This Book Came About

Lifelong friends Dan and Angelo were discussing the merits and tactics of intermittent fasting. It was a system they were both using to control their diet, enhance their mental clarity, and improve their health. Angelo suggested that the mindfulness gained from fasting had positive practical implications on many aspects of his own life and wondered if it would apply toward Dan's profession.

Could the benefits of intermittent fasting apply to personal finance? The conversation quickly jumped from restricting eating to restricting spending. This marked the beginning of what has now become intermittent spending and The Spending Window™. After years of experimenting with and observing different intermittent spending tactics, Dan and Angelo finally put their strategy on paper in hopes that people around the world will become more mindful of their spending behavior.

Copyright © 2020 The Spending Window, Inc.
All rights reserved.
ISBN: 9798569151615

CONTENTS

Introduction   4

Chapter One – Money Problems   8

Chapter Two – Intermittent Spending   25

Chapter Three – The Spending Window™   41

Chapter Four – Measuring Progress   60

Chapter Five – COVID-19   71

Chapter Six – Sticky Money   88

Chapter Seven – 10 Common Pitfalls   103

Conclusion   119

Intermittent Spending: *the act of positively changing our spending habits by abstaining from spending during a specific timeframe.*

Spending Window™: *the timeframe during which we allow ourselves to spend money.*

Introduction
Meet Kim and Joe

I would like to introduce you to a couple I know. The spouses, Kim and Joe, are 40 years old and live in a suburb of New York City. The couple have two children, ages 11 and 8. They both work, and their combined annual income totals $110,000.

For many people, this is no small amount of money. In their neighborhood, however, Kim and Joe are considered middle-class. This is in large part due to their location. Living so close to the City can be expensive. There's lots of pressure to keep up with the Joneses. Plus, neither Kim nor Joe come from a wealthy family, and they don't have much in the way of retirement savings.

Now, Kim and Joe have about $15,000 in their checking account. This allows them to cover monthly expenses and maintain reasonable cash flow.

On the other hand, they also have a sizcable mortgage and over $150,000 in student loan debt.

This means that each month, Kim and Joe are barely covering their bills. They aren't adding much to their savings outside of their 401(k)-salary match. And while they have tried to create a budget, they find the process frustrating.

You see, Kim and Joe don't like micromanaging each other's expenses. It makes them uneasy, worrying about every little thing they buy. And while they don't yet blame each other for their financial woes, it looks like things might move in that direction if they don't take action quickly.

They have tried to create a budget—but both Kim and Joe find this process frustrating. They simply don't know which areas to cut back on their spending. It's a real struggle, because Kim and Joe want to stay in their current house and neighborhood. Even though their mortgage, insurance, and taxes eat up a large part of their finances, they aren't ready to make drastic lifestyle changes.

They aren't even necessarily ready to make *less* drastic changes. Both spouses maintain up-to-date work wardrobes that they find necessary. And they don't want to spare any expense on their kids' schooling or extracurricular activities.

Yet each time they look at their budget and overall expenditures, Kim and Joe agree their finances look overwhelming. Since there are no obvious expenses they can cut, they resign themselves to barely scraping by. Kim and Joe decide instead—in an effort to break free from this financial treadmill—to focus instead on increasing their income. But in reality, they recognize that any salary increases will quickly be eaten up by new expenditures for their family. Either that, or they'll go toward paying off debts.

Nonetheless, Kim and Joe are aware that something needs to change. But since they are not spending more than they make, they do not have enough financial pain to fully embrace a traditional financial planning and budgeting process.

They still aren't saving much, if anything. So, Kim and Joe sit down and discuss their goals, and they jointly determine they want to increase their savings account from $0 to $25,000 within a year. To achieve this, they agree to cut their expenses—noting that their salaries won't increase enough to fill the gap.

They came upon the idea of a Spending Window™. Intermittent spending, they decide, will help to force a sense of mindfulness. The couple believe that this kind of custom approach will put them on a better financial path. And so, they start planning their own personalized window.

Kim and Joe begin with a 16:8 Spending Window™, which we'll discuss in more detail in Chapter Three (along with other common window shapes and sizes). Since the spouses work full-time, they figure they can make a real difference by eliminating their morning expenditures. So, they commit to only spend their money between noon and 8 p.m. each day—even on weekends.

As you'll learn in the pages that follow, it's important to take things in stride while navigating your intermittent spending journey—to make changes along the way. You don't want your window to give you *too* much leeway, but conversely, you shouldn't deny yourself all the things and experiences you enjoy. Your Spending Window™ should be just flexible enough to fit in your life.

Kim and Joe decide to try their new window for a month and then revisit its size and structure. Before they begin, they gather their bank and credit card statements, their online payment transaction history (platforms may vary, but these two use Venmo), and start looking at where their money has been going. Rather than analyzing the validity of their expenses, they commit to taking an objective look at the payments they've been making.

Here is what they find: Kim is primarily responsible for their household's major payments, including their mortgage, insurance, taxes, childcare, and other recurring expenses. She decides to leave those items alone; she and Joe agree that these are necessary items on which they cannot compromise.

The automated expenses under Joe's jurisdiction, on the other hand? Those they can take a closer look at. Kim and Joe decide to pause their gym membership, their online movie and music subscriptions, their video game subscription, and more. They determine that instead of making recurring payments on these nonessential items, they can discuss each expense in real time and make manual payments on a case-by-case basis. For instance, Joe claims the family gym membership is an essential expense—but in the spirit of intermittent spending, he'll consider the expense each month before swiping his card.

This, both Kim and Joe find, will encourage mindfulness. It will also improve their communication. The spouses start to feel confident in their process. They commit to a $20 cash allowance for purchases inside their window, and they set a zero-tolerance policy of expenditures outside their Spending Window™.

Finally, Kim and Joe are ready to dive headfirst into intermittent spending. Their window is set, and they are eager to get started.

You can do the same thing as Kim and Joe. The results may well astound you. And this book will teach you everything you need to know about curating your own intermittent spending experience and creating your own Spending Window™. At the end of the text, we'll check in with Kim and Joe. I won't give too much away, but I will say that several months in, they're very happy they took the plunge.

Chapter One
Money Problems
Spotlight on Spending

In my years of retirement planning, I've observed something very interesting.

Basically, we've got it all wrong.

Now, I have a background in financial planning, investment management, and retirement income planning. I understand that money is important, and that it plays an essential role in our society.

But for the most part, when people come to me for the first time, they ask how much money they *need* for their retirement. "Is $1 million enough?" they may ask. "Is $2 million enough?" These people want to plan their retirement with a specific dollar amount in mind. They often think there's a magic number that will allow them to live out their retirement dreams.

Of course, people want to protect the money they have. They want to invest their assets and ensure the best possible return on their investments. And while this is all well and good, I'd like to let you in on a little secret: These people aren't looking at the full picture.

A Broken System
Based on what I've witnessed in my profession, money isn't the main driver of success. Our spending habits, though? Those are a different story.

Personally, I would rather have clients come to me with little saved—yet be in control of their spending—than approach me with a large retirement nest egg and no control of their spending.

So why, then, do we tend to focus on money? First, planning for retirement based on a specific dollar amount is the way it's always been. And two, the business model for financial advisors typically includes a fee based on a percentage of the client's assets. This means it's in the advisor's best interest for the client to have more money. More money saved means more money spent on products your financial advisor gets commissions on, or a higher fee based on a larger asset.

Admittedly, this is the way things often are in my industry. But when it comes to helping others with seemingly complex situations—like retirement or general financial planning—I value safety and simplicity. Lots of my colleagues do as well. And I think that above all else, people need to go back to the source of their money challenges and look at what matters most.

They need to take a look at their spending habits.

It All Comes Down to Spending
It's simple, really: Our spending dictates how much money we have. People can ask how much money they need for, say, their retirement. But the answer is almost always that they need *more*.

Even in high-earning professions like medicine and law, many workers feel they never have enough money. In fact, these higher earners may at times be less financially stable than those who make a quarter of what they do—all because of how much money they spend.

At the end of the day, people usually want more. They might earn a nice income and, rather than putting more money away, they buy a second home, or a third car, or they spend their money on more lavish vacations. And the next thing they know, the amount of money they "need" has increased—and they're no better off.

We can control our income, but only to an extent. For instance, doctors can control their income by investing in their education. They can go through college, and complete medical school and their residencies, and then pass their boards before launching their practice and doing a good job.

But ultimately, there's a limit to how much we can earn. People can ask for a raise (although many of them don't). They can't, however, guarantee an exponential increase in their earnings.

So, what *can* we control? We can control how much we spend. This includes our basic necessities: food, shelter, fuel to get to and from work—you get the gist of it. Yet, there's a lack of awareness in this country. Few people realize they may need to reevaluate their spending patterns.

Breaking Those Harmful Spending Habits
Now, I've spoken some about retirement planning in this book. However, people at any life stage can learn from the content in these pages. The only criterion is this: You must be open to the idea of getting your spending under control.

The big thing, where retirement planning is concerned, is that you need to start saving when you're young. You need to save early and get that compounding interest and start putting money away in your 20s, so it'll be there and waiting for you—exponentially bigger—decades later.[1]

But few people do this because they want their money now. And the same thing can be said about spending. I would suggest that the earlier you can get your spending under control, the better off you'll be.

Awareness is the first step. Most people don't actually know how much they spend. Generally speaking, though, I would say people spend more money than they should. It's out of control—and in many ways, I believe this can be traced back to the debt issues we have in our country.

A National Debt Problem
Take a deep breath for a moment. I'm going to share with you how much debt the United States government has accumulated.

In July 2020, as of the writing of this book, our national debt totaled $26,509,696,627,544.92.[2]

You heard me right—that's over $26 *trillion* of national debt. By 2028, some say we can expect upwards of $78 trillion of national debt.[3] And this epidemic has seeped into our culture in many ways. U.S. citizens, just like our government, have on average much more debt than they really should. In May 2020, consumer debt featured a record-breaking total of $14.3 trillion.[4]

---

[1] See a detailed discussion on this in Chapter Five.
[2] treasurydirect.gov/govt/reports/pd/pd_debttothepenny.htm

[3] forbes.com/sites/mikepatton/2020/08/14/national-debt-to-surpass-78-trillion-by-2028-what-it-means-for-americans/
[4] cnbc.com/2020/05/05/consumer-debt-hits-new-record-of-14point3-trillion.html

That's a decent chunk of change. And again, that figure doesn't include home mortgages. So many Americans are dealing with even more debt on top of that amount. Based on what I've seen in my profession—and based on what my peers have shared with me—I have reason to believe debt is rooted in our culture.

Keeping Up with the Joneses
Have you noticed that as people start to earn more income, they start to spend more? There's an impulse for many of us to show off our wealth—to "keep up with the Joneses," if you will. We're bombarded with cultural messages to buy bigger houses, purchase nicer toys (boats and snowmobiles, to name a few), lease higher-end cars, and simply spend above our means to maintain an image of prosperity.

Who Are the Joneses?

The phrase "Keeping Up with the Joneses" has exploded in contemporary pop culture. The title of a star-studded 2016 film, it also inspired the name of several songs and the infamous reality show Keeping Up with the Kardashians.

But where did it come from? The concept of "Keeping Up with the Joneses" actually dates back more than a century—to a 1913 Arthur "Pop" Momand cartoon that ran in the New York World *until 1938.*

The strip featured the McGinis family, a group of social climbers, who were desperate to keep up with their neighbors, the Joneses. Today you might find that many of us have metaphorical Joneses we consciously, or subconsciously, compete with.

nytimes.com/1998/11/15/magazine/on-language-up-the-down-ladder.html

Think about the word *image* for a moment. It has elusive connotations. I mean, what are we trying to prove? And typically, keeping up with the Joneses isn't a problem that affects people who are just scraping by. This is because minimum wage earners and those living paycheck to paycheck are simply trying to keep their heads above water.

On the other hand, people who *do* have extra money are only rarely saving it. Most are too busy trying to keep up with the Joneses.

This phenomenon is also known as lifestyle creep. The more we earn, the more many of us feel we need to spend—and so we spend more. And we spend *more*. And the cycle continues until we find ourselves no better off than we were when we were earning less money.

Want to buy a bigger house? By doing so, you'll pay higher taxes. You'll be on the hook for higher utility bills. You'll also be dealing with a major spike in maintenance costs should anything go wrong. A bigger house means a more expensive roof repair, a steeper bill from the painter. So, maybe you don't want to buy a bigger house after all—but how can you keep up with the Joneses if you don't live in the "right" neighborhood?

It's a vicious cycle. Far too many people link their self-worth to their material possessions. We're hammered with this from all angles on a daily basis. On TV, on the radio, even in internet pop-up ads—people are bombarded with the idea that there's this ideal life. The luxury cars, the white picket fence, the 2.2 kids, the dog, the whole nine yards—these things are rooted in our spending habits. The problem is psychological, because there is a great deal of pressure to keep up with the Joneses.

Credit Card Companies: A Common Trap
It's a tough pill to swallow, but it's the truth: Financial organizations are profiting off of our lack of spending control. Credit card companies are making it easy for us to part with our money—by giving people access to money they don't have.

How so?

Consider the following study conducted by the Financial Industry Regulatory Authority (FINRA), a self-regulatory agency I deal with often in my profession. This 2016 report compares how much people are spending to how much they are making. It's called the "Investor Education Foundation: Financial Capability in the United States" report.[5]

The results of the report astounded me. I think you'll find them equally impactful. In essence, the report revealed that only 40% of Americans were spending less than they were bringing in at the time. This means that less than half the United States population was earning more than they were spending!

What does that say about the rest of the country? Well, 41% of Americans were spending the same amount they were bringing in—living paycheck to paycheck, if you will—and 19% were actually spending more money than they were making.

Believe me when I say that credit card companies are happy to help people achieve this.

---

[5] usfinancialcapability.org/downloads/NFCS_2018_Report_Natl_Findings.pdf

The Perils of Spending on Credit

When you spend money on credit, you don't actually have the physical dollars in hand. Yet, people tend to use credit like a bank account. Some believe the money they have on credit is theirs to do with as they please. The problem, however, is that many of these people don't have the money they need when it comes time to pay their credit card bill. This tends to snowball into more debt—and people must pay interest on their debt.

From there, the cycle spirals further out of control. These individuals dig themselves deeper and deeper into a bottomless hole of sorts, and they accumulate even more debt.

There's a simple solution, though. That solution is to stop overspending. But is it really that easy?

It all boils down to a couple of simple questions. Questions that people—particularly those who spend using credit—should ask themselves.

These questions include:

1. **Should you even have those credit cards?**
2. **Are your credit limits higher than they should be?**

Now, you can ask yourself these questions. But your responses to these questions must come from within. You shouldn't simply see an ad for a new credit card, and then respond by mindlessly filling out an application. You shouldn't open your mailbox, and then jump the gun on a brand-new card just because you've been preapproved for a certain limit.

Instead, you should be suspicious of those offers. You should take a minute to acknowledge that those credit card companies are looking to *profit* off consumers who like to spend money using credit. So now, it's up to each individual to put an end to this because the credit card companies aren't going to change—at least not right away. Therefore we, as a society, need to maintain some semblance of self-control.

Birthdays and Bonuses
Did you enjoy your birthday as a kid? Maybe you still do but think back to when you were young. Chances are you looked forward to celebrating with friends and family, indulging in a thick slice of cake, and unwrapping a generous pile of gifts.

Now, think back for a moment to those gifts. Was there ever a time, a month or two before your birthday, that you saw something you really wanted to buy? A sleek-looking bike, maybe, or a video game, or a brand-new guitar or drum kit?

Did you ever ask your parents to buy you the gift you so desired? You might have asked them to buy it for you on "credit." Your birthday, after all, was still a couple months away. So, if you wanted that gift immediately, you may have had to leverage the purchase against a future birthday present.

"If you get me this now, you won't have to get me anything for my birthday," you might have told Mom or Dad.

So, your parents bought you the gift. You brought it home, and you were thrilled to ride that bike or play those drums or do whatever it was that gift allowed you to do. And then, the day of your birthday, you likely found yourself disappointed that there was no big present to unwrap.

Much like spending money using credit, you were seeking instant gratification at the expense of a future reward. This behavior is pretty typical, and we tend to learn it from an early age.

This reminds me of the Stanford Marshmallow Experiment.[6] You've probably heard of this famous study.

Here's the gist of it. Conducted in the early 1970s, researchers took young children one at a time into a room with a single marshmallow on display. They told the children to sit right in front of the marshmallow. Then, before leaving the room, the researchers told the kids they'd receive a second marshmallow—*if* and only if they didn't eat the first one in their absence. The experiment revealed that the kids who waited wound up earning higher scores on standardized tests and doing better in life in general when they got older.

So, what does delayed gratification say about us? There might be an inherent bias toward delayed gratification in some kids. Maybe there's a genetic or an emotional disposition to be more impulsive—but I think what we're finding, and what I've seen through my work, is that societally speaking, we're more impulsive than we should be. It's catching up with us.

Another important consideration is that these behaviors don't necessarily end in adulthood. Even today, you might

---

[6] semanticscholar.org/paper/Attention-in-Delay-of-Gratification.-Mischel-Ebbesen/29346b98f0947a822b8744f4792bcf1a297f01d3

expect a $20,000 annual bonus from your job. Anticipating this bonus, you may spend $15,000 on a lavish vacation to the Bahamas—months before you receive the money.

But then, the bonus never comes. It's been a rough year for your firm, and there's simply no cash flow for bonuses.

What happens, then, if you've already spent the funds you were counting on? What if the money you spent was money you didn't have? Even if you did have the funds, what if you failed to spend mindfully? Even if the bonus is received as expected, will there be some level of regret that the funds should be used in a different way due to new circumstances?

More Money Is Not Always the Answer
It's important to have money. We can't just go through life and not have money. We need to feed our families, keep the lights on in our homes, and fuel up so we can go to work. We should be aware of the fact, however, that having more money does not necessarily translate to a higher quality of life.

For years now, I've witnessed people inherit money, and I've found those funds never last long. The problem isn't really about how much money people inherit, but about how willingly they spend the cash.

Without the right mindset—without healthy habits—our spending can get out of control fast.

You might consider lottery winners as well. Scour the internet, and you'll come across striking headlines like "20 lottery winners who lost every penny,"[7] "A Treasury of

---

[7] businessinsider.com/lottery-winners-lost-everything-2017-8

Terribly Sad Stories of Lotto Winners,"[8] and "Here's How Winning the Lottery Makes You Miserable."[9] These are gripping pieces published by sources like *The Atlantic* and *Time*. They too reveal that our financial health can be traced back to our spending habits.

Think of it like a diet. Rather than counting calories, or budgeting your money to the dollar, we can work toward an overarching shift in the way we view our finances. We can transform our financial habits, start spending mindfully, and embark on a journey of delayed gratification.

Delayed Gratification: It's a Virtue
Financial literacy, to my disappointment, isn't a core component of the American education system. This means most people simply aren't taught to save the way they should be saving, let alone spend appropriately. They start making poor spending decisions early in life. A lot of kids have this problem. They just spend money on a whim, without thinking about the impact of their actions.

There's a lack of delayed gratification in our culture, which means there's this notion that we can always start saving "later." But when is "later"? Why on Earth shouldn't people learn to save as soon as they start earning money?

From my perspective, people's spending habits tend to be questionable from the beginning of adulthood. This leads them to accumulate much more debt than they should be accumulating. A simple tool to help with delayed

---

[8] theatlantic.com/national/archive/2012/03/terribly-sad-true-stories-lotto-winners/329903/
[9] time.com/4176128/powerball-jackpot-lottery-winners/

gratification is to approach an expense by categorizing it as a need versus a want.

So instead of focusing on how much money you *can* spend, consider exploring how much money you *need to* spend. Rather than looking into how much house you can *afford*—or what mortgage you qualify for—you might assess how big a house you *need*.

Now let's talk about student loan debt. Student loan debt is considered "good debt," but it's still debt—so you need to have some understanding of it. To this end, many are graduating from college with an immense amount of debt, which leaves them behind the eight ball when they graduate. For this reason, I believe the decision to take on a college loan is made much too lightly.

When people decide on what degree to get, or whether they ought to be getting one at all, they should be researching the potential return on their investment.

Should they be getting a degree in something that's going to yield a high return? Should they lean toward a higher salary, or should they instead study something they simply love to do? These are important questions people should be asking from a young age.

The Broken Windows Theory
We've talked about some of the major spending choices that get people into trouble. Next, I'm going to talk about some of the smaller financial decisions we make—including the impact they have on the bigger picture.

Of course, I'm not going to insist that you give up the lattes you so enjoy. At least not altogether. But cutting back—preparing your own coffee at home or at the office most mornings, and only picking up an artisanal drink a couple times per week—could serve you well.

Let's take a step back for a moment. To fix our big spending problems, and to build positive habits, we must move incrementally in the right direction. We have to make thoughtful decisions. By doing so, we can create meaningful, lasting changes.

This will help us change our whole environment and address the collective spending problems we face in this country.

How so? Consider the broken windows theory. I used to work in New York City. I remember when former Mayor Rudy Giuliani started fixing the broken windows in certain neighborhoods, in an effort to get the city crime down. This was in the early 1990s, about 10 years after *The Atlantic* published an article called "Broken Windows" on this exact topic.[10] Giuliani subscribed to the theory that if criminals were to see a broken window, they'd be more likely to commit a crime in the area. In neighborhoods free of broken windows, though, they might think twice.

The interesting thing about the broken windows theory is that it doesn't matter whether the neighborhood is nice or a bit more rundown—the psychology behind the theory is consistent throughout. This is because, according to authors James Q. Wilson and George L. Kelling, the repaired windows signal that people *care*.

And so, by being intentional with money not only in terms of how much we need, but also regarding how much we *spend*, we too can fix the broken windows in our financial

---

[10] theatlantic.com/magazine/archive/1982/03/broken-windows/304465/

lives. By being aware of common issues, and by harnessing our spending before it gets out of control, we can increase awareness and keep those windows intact.

Maybe we need to look at our spending as many small windows. By fixing even the smallest windows, one at a time, we can spark an overall positive change. And we can encourage others to do the same.

Intentional Spending
Jonah is a financial analyst. He makes approximately $200,000 per year, and he spends his full salary on new suits, fancy cars, a nice apartment, and so on. Jonah spends right up to the limit of what he makes after taxes.

I can always earn more; he thinks each time he splurges on a major purchase. *I'll just make more to cover this.*

Then there's Niko, who brings in $50,000 per year as an associate professor. He too is a big spender and lives paycheck to paycheck.

Who is better off: Jonah or Niko?

The truth is that the higher earner is no better off than the lower earner—or vice versa—if neither person is saving money. Both professionals are on a treadmill of sorts. They're running with these zero balances, and that's exactly the problem. There's a lack of intentionality in the way they spend their money.

Now, clients often tell me, "I wish I'd saved more." They might say, "I wish I'd held on to that," or, "I wish I'd done things differently with my investments."

Rarely do I hear them say, "I wish I'd spent less money when I was young."

I think this is because people don't want to admit they weren't intentional with their spending in their 20s. I also think people just love to spend their money. There's a lot of mindless spending going on, and before people know it, they're in a hole. It can be tough to come to terms with this.

Again, this doesn't mean you need to stop spending money on things you enjoy. College students work hard, and most of them want to go away for spring break. They should be able to do this if they so choose. Similarly, parents work hard, and they may want to splurge on a second home or leave the country for a vacation.

If these things matter to you, then they absolutely are important—but you need understand the impact they have on your spending. This is where this book comes in. We're going to spend some time covering topics like the Spending Window™, and the importance of awareness and mindful spending habits.

If you think about it, the major issues we face as a country—the lack of money and social security, the trillions of dollars of national debt—these are all due to a lack of delayed gratification.

If we as individuals work on this, eventually we can shape our society to be a little bit different. You may find that when you work on yourself, your efforts will touch your family members, and then your colleagues, and before you know it, you'll be a part of something bigger.

So, join the movement. Start with yourself because we're all connected. You've already taken the first step by picking up this book. In the next chapter, we'll focus on mindfulness, and the role mindful thinking plays in financial success.

By really focusing on what we can control—by being *mindful*—we can do better in the way we spend and save money.

Chapter Two
Intermittent Spending
A Financial Approach to Mindfulness

Let's talk about mindfulness. You don't have to go very far these days to come across mindfulness and its different applications.

Merriam Webster defines mindfulness as *the practice of maintaining a nonjudgmental state of heightened or complete awareness of one's thoughts, emotions, or experiences on a moment-to-moment basis.*[11] Basically, mindfulness involves being aware of what we're doing, when we're doing it, and why. It's traditionally played an important role in eastern philosophy, and it's gained immense popularity in the western world as well.

Today we might speak of mindfulness in relation to eating; in relation to stress, anxiety, or even insomnia reduction; or in relation to improvements in one's overall health.

We might also speak of mindfulness in relation to our spending habits. But when it comes to behavioral finance, there's a huge void where mindfulness is concerned. There isn't much out there on the topic of mindful spending.

This brings us to the meat of this book: intermittent spending. In this chapter, I am going to outline the parallels between our spending habits and our eating habits, and touch on how we can embrace mindfulness and make changes in the way we view and spend money.

---

[11] merriam-webster.com/dictionary/mindfulness

Eating, Spending, and Governing the Emotions
We tend to eat when we're emotional. If we aren't mindful of what we're eating, we'll likely eat more than we would otherwise. There are also some parallels that show how eating in a group environment tends to result in eating more (in many cases, to the point of overeating).

Spending works the same way in that we typically spend more money in a social setting. We may spend too much money. We may spend money when, under other circumstances, we wouldn't spend any money at all. This is because when we're emotional, we generally think less about how we spend our hard-earned cash.

When we do anything to excess—when we overeat, or overspend, or drink too much—our behavior is rooted in the emotions. So, by governing our feelings, we can make tremendous gains in our personal well-being. More specifically, using mindfulness to regulate the emotions can lead to improvements in everything from a person's career and family life, to their waistline and bank account.

Just think about it: While in Chapter One we focused on keeping up with the Joneses and the societal pressures we face, there's also a situational aspect to spending.

When you're at a restaurant or a bar or even an amusement park, chances are you're not even aware of how much you're putting on your credit card. Right? You're being social, your emotions are activated, and you're likely spending without putting much thought into it.

This lack of mindfulness is exactly what spawned the idea of intermittent spending.

Let's go back to the link between eating and spending for a moment. In addition to spending and becoming more and more in debt, we, as a society, are also becoming overweight. And when it comes to addressing the obesity crisis, several experts have turned to intermittent fasting.

While conceptually speaking intermittent fasting has caught on in modern culture, it too is a tale as old as time. Just look in the Bible, and you'll find that intermittent fasting goes way back.[12] Still today, fasting is a part of many religions.

To this end, I think the best way to talk about intermittent spending is to relate it to the concept of intermittent fasting—and to build on that analogy.

So, consider the following definitions:

Intermittent Fasting: *the act of transforming our eating habits by abstaining from eating during a specific timeframe (or timeframes), and then eating as we would normally.*[13]

Intermittent Spending: *the act of positively changing our spending habits by abstaining from spending during a specific timeframe (or timeframes), and then spending as we would normally.*

It's all about limiting the time we eat, or the time we spend money. And it seems so straightforward, yet we just don't do these things as a society. However, after researching—and experiencing firsthand—the benefits of both intermittent fasting and intermittent spending, I believe

---

[12] bible.org/question/what-does-bible-say-about-fasting
[13] medicalnewstoday.com/articles/322293

these solutions are great alternatives to traditional dieting and budgeting. There's a vast correlation between the two from which I think we can learn a great deal. More often than not, traditional dieting and traditional budgeting just don't work.

Where Traditional Diets (and Budgets) Fall Short
When I first started researching intermittent fasting, I turned to Dr. Jason Fung—a Canadian nephrologist and the author of bestselling books *The Obesity Code* and *The Complete Guide to Fasting*.[14,15] One of the findings that stood out to me in Fung's research was that the vast majority of fad diets fail.

Fad diets may work for a bit in the short term. They just aren't a viable long-term solution because they aren't sustainable! As Fung explains, there's a reason the hit weight-loss TV show *The Biggest Loser* doesn't air reunion episodes.

The reason for this is that the idea of "eat less, exercise more" doesn't work—at least not as a standalone strategy. People might slip up. They might lose track of their progress and revert to old habits. They might feel overwhelmed by a perceived lack of control that simply doesn't exist with intermittent fasting.

Conversely, intermittent fasting can be very successful.

Why doesn't this lack of control exist with intermittent fasting? Because intermittent fasting focuses on when we eat! It forces us to be mindful without having to consider

---

[14] amazon.com/Obesity-Code-Unlocking-Secrets-Weight/dp/1536682187
[15] amazon.com/Complete-Guide-Fasting-Intermittent-Alternate-Day/dp/1628600012

how we might hold ourselves accountable. And intermittent spending works the same way.

Traditional budgeting is similar to dieting and calorie counting. Budgeting is important, just like what you eat is important. However, it is difficult to not only create a budget, but to stick to it as well. Many people give up early. Traditional dieting is to budgeting what intermittent fasting is to intermittent spending.

It's All About Limiting *When* You Spend
Read the above subtitle one more time. Ingrain it in your memory.

Now, look at your relationship with your credit card. When is the last time you really thought about it?

Think about when you reach for your Visa or your American Express. Think about what you tend to buy, and about what compels you to buy what you buy.

If ever you've made a purchase that in hindsight you felt was ill-advised, think about what was going on in your life at the time. Were there emotional factors that might have made you more prone to that spending decision?

Chances are that yes, there were. These are key considerations you might reflect on before you begin your intermittent spending program. These are things that could translate to huge changes, if only you take a moment to consider them.

The problem, though, is that while people may contemplate what they spend their money on, most don't reflect on *when* they spend their money. They don't stop to think about the driving forces behind their decision-making.

Truth be told, those driving forces aren't always clear. People often make the decision to spend in the moment.

Spending can be very impulsive—and that often leads to trouble. It's just like impulsive eating. If you eat without being mindful, and without thinking about when you're eating, you may well run into trouble. You'll gain weight if you eat compulsively over a prolonged period of time. If you focus on *when* you eat, however, you can gain better control of your overall eating habits.

You see, counting calories is a losing game because no one wants to do it. No one likes counting calories. No one! It's painful for people to sit around and fixate on what they're eating. Because people don't like counting calories, they'll count them for a month and see some results—but then they'll get tired of tracking every morsel of food they put in their mouths, because counting calories just isn't practical.

But limiting *when* you take in calories, on the other hand? That's a lot easier to manage. You set the alarm clock. You know the time window, or windows, during which you aren't meant to eat. You get used to a pattern. Most importantly, you don't have to *think* about it all the time. You just eat within your window, and that's that. In this way, intermittent fasting is designed to hold the person accountable and spark positive behavioral change.

The same thing applies to budgeting. Budgeting is a four-letter word, if you understand what I mean. Tracking every dollar you spend just doesn't work. Most people don't want to create a budget; they don't want to have to *think* about budgeting. It's much easier to just use that credit card and spend away. But with intermittent spending, you simply limit *when* you spend. I'd like to take a moment to share an example of someone who did just that.

Insights from My Client John
I'd like to tell you the story of one of my most interesting clients. Let's call him John.

John is 59 years old. He is divorced from his first wife and happily married to Robyn, with whom he has two teenage daughters. John also has two adult children from his prior marriage.

A lawyer in a successful private law firm, John's income has skyrocketed over the years, currently topping $700,000. But as his earnings have grown, so have his expenses. John put his two older kids through college, giving them access to an expensive education. He then put his eldest through medical school, and he is now putting his second-oldest child through law school. His younger daughters attend costly private schools.

John works very hard. He also values his leisure time. And when he is not working, he likes to enjoy himself—sparing no expense. John lives in a high-end suburb near his law firm. When he takes Robyn and his kids on vacation, they stay at exotic, all-inclusive resorts. John also leases a luxury sedan through his corporate account, and he enjoys a convertible outside of work hours. He even splurged on an expensive custom motorcycle.

In addition, John has been spending more and more time in Florida. He recently purchased a condominium he and his family use two weeks per year, though they try to rent it out the rest of the time. More recently, when John and Robyn decided to change things up and visit Hawaii, the successful lawyer decided to purchase a timeshare on his favorite island.

It may sound like John is doing very well financially—and he's certainly leading an impressive lifestyle. Despite earning an income that would easily put him in the top 1% of all Americans, however, my client is struggling to stay afloat. Financial stress has been taking a toll on him, and John often finds himself worrying about his rising expenses. Some time ago, his company faced an unexpected downturn, and John had to borrow from his retirement to cover his bills. At his current trajectory, he will be unable to retire before the age of 70—yet he already feels the stress is wearing him down.

John told me as much about a year ago. From my vantage point, I could tell right away that even though he drove the nicest cars, ate at the fanciest restaurants, and kept pictures of his family at the most exotic vacation sites on his desk, John was having a rough go of it. In our initial hour-long consultation, he must have mentioned his 80-hour workweek four or five times.

Now, one of the first things I do when I meet with a client for the first time is ask them about their goals. When I spoke with John, he told me his main goal was "financial freedom."

I could tell he needed some help where that goal was concerned. It became apparent to me that John's expensive vacations, designer clothing, and restaurant meals were expenditures he made during periods of stress—typically when my client was feeling overworked. He was using these material items to compensate for being overwhelmed. Yet eventually, the cost of these trips caught up with him, making him feel he needed to work even harder to make ends meet. This resulted in greater stress than ever, effectively perpetuating the cycle.

As many of us know, awareness is the first step. John knew he had to make a change. To mitigate his financial stress, he and I came up with a rudimentary Spending Window™. Immediately, John began to reap the benefits of intermittent spending.

We started with a generous window of eight hours per day, seven days per week. The key with John was to strategically time the window so that he wouldn't be quite so stressed at work when he was allowed to spend. It did not take long before he became aware of the correlation between his stress and his spending. He realized that when he was calm and collected, he made more intelligent financial decisions. This quickly resulted in less impulsive spending.

Today John is much more mindful of his spending habits. He can recognize which investments really matter to him—like his children's schooling—and which ones he can go without. John tells me he and Robyn are happier than ever, in large part because he is much less stressed.

John credits these improvements to his custom Spending Window™. You can too. Be sure to build yours with lasting, sustainable results in mind.

Time Restriction and Sustainability
The goal is to be more mindful of your spending, right?

Without a system in place, it isn't quite so easy. You can't simply wake up one morning and decide to be mindful.

You wouldn't tell an obese person to just stop eating. You wouldn't approach an alcoholic and tell them to just stop drinking.

It's not that easy!

While it isn't impossible—far from it—it isn't quite so simple. This is because people need to break their patterns. An empowering, effective way to break a pattern is through time restriction.

It's a lot easier to overcome the urge to do something when you know it's not in your eating or Spending Window™.

The idea here is sustainability. This book isn't designed to be some sort of easy money-saving or "get rich quick" scheme. We all know schemes don't work in the long-term. If they did, everyone would be turning to them!

I'll repeat myself: You can't just walk up to someone and tell them not to eat any sweets. You can't just tell someone to stop drinking alcohol—to go through a detox period and be done with drinking. You also can't just tell someone to stop spending without giving them a tool to do so. People may be able to break their patterns for a certain period of time, but they'll struggle to make sustainable, long-term changes by going cold turkey. And sustainable changes are exactly the type of changes we're hoping to make.

Your Financial Health Is Not a Sprint
You know the difference between a sprint and a marathon, right?

Well, fad diets and template budgets are sprints. They aren't designed to be long-lasting. This is why you should treat your financial well-being like a marathon—like an *ultra-marathon*. That's what's going to translate to long-term financial health.

I could tell you to try to be more mindful, and the rest will come. But again, intermittent spending isn't quite so easy. This is why I'm going to offer some guidelines that will *force* that mindfulness. A set of easy-to-follow rules will make this intermittent spending platform a whole lot easier and much more palatable.

Say you tell someone, "Stop eating dessert!"

How effective do you think that will be? They might skip the bakery run for a week or two, but more likely than not, they'll revert to old habits.

Say you tell someone, "Stop eating dessert between noon and 2 p.m."

That's a lot easier to handle. Rather than feeling as though they're depriving themselves, people will feel like they're simply managing the timing of *when* they indulge. And still, by doing so—by taking control in this way—the results will likely follow.

So, I urge you to start there with your spending. To create a Spending Window™, no matter how small. (We'll go over this in more detail in the next chapter.) Once you get started, you can open that window a little more, and a little more again, and eventually you'll reach a point where you can eliminate those sweets altogether.

By focusing on the timing aspect of when you eat—and the timing aspect of when you spend—you will automatically become more aware. You will automatically cut out those sweets, or whatever it is you're hoping to cut back on. You will automatically start budgeting. You'll become more mindful without feeling restricted or forced into a mindfulness practice you didn't ask for.

Intermittent Spending: A Synergistic Formula
Personally, I'm excited to give people the formula for how this works. I'm eager to get into the recipe for intermittent spending success, so to speak. Time and time again, I've seen how small changes can transform people's lives. Just take a look at John from our earlier example.

If you're mindful of your spending, you'll be in a better position to improve your overall well-being: your physical health, your mental health, and even your financial health. Intermittent spending is synergistic in this way. It's meant to be a long-term solution.

The idea is to push past impulsivity—to avoid faltering. In theory, everyone wants to strengthen their retirement portfolio, right? The answer is a resounding yes. And so, when people go astray, initially there's a strong emotional reaction.

In a healthcare setting, people might say, "Oh no, I have cancer. I'll do whatever it takes to beat it." Or, if they're facing some sort of obesity-related condition, they'll say, "I'll do what I need to do to lose weight."

Why, then, do so many people have such a hard time staying on track?

The answer is that while their intention might be there, that intention needs to be sustained. And it isn't always easy to sustain that intention because life will always, always get in the way. We can't predict the future.

Today your physical health, or your financial focus, might be your number-one priority. But then tomorrow, life may throw something at you. You may fall off-balance as a result. Something within will have *shifted*. The only way to stay on track, whether it's dealing with a health problem or a financial problem, is to have a system in place. It helps to have a formula like intermittent spending at your disposal.

Our formula here isn't overbearing. It's simple and easy to implement. You can work within the framework under any circumstances—even during those times life throws you a curveball.

Eliminate Decisions, Eliminate Stress
I think of intermittent spending as a fast. Creating a personalized Spending Window™ is the answer for many people. This is because, like intermittent fasting, it takes away a lot of the second-guessing involved in making an important lifestyle change.

It removes a lot of the decision-making we face—a lot of the pressure we may experience. Because let's face it: People make poor decisions from time to time. Particularly, as I've found in my line of work, we make poor decisions where money is concerned.

A key reason for this is that we can only handle a certain amount of stimuli at any given time. In this day and age, you may think you can handle multitasking and a bunch of things coming at you from all different directions—but there's only so much you can take at once. If you're buried at work, and one of your kids is having a hard time in school, and your car needs to be serviced, and you're grappling with a sick parent, you'll undeniably have a lot on your plate. You don't need to add even more complexity to your life.

So, why not reduce the number of decisions you have to make each day?

Just think about some of the nation's most successful people: music mogul Dr. Dre, former president Barack Obama, and tech pioneers Mark Zuckerberg and the late Steve Jobs.

What do these individuals have in common?

They've all been vocal about limiting their wardrobe to a certain color or style. This, they believe, has helped to increase their productivity, and reduce their stress—all by decreasing the number of decisions they're forced to make each day.[16]

Dr. Dre sports the same shoes every day (Nike Air Force 1s in case you were wondering).

Obama, during his presidency, wore only gray or blue suits.

Facebook founder Mark Zuckerberg, meanwhile, enjoys gray Brunello Cucinelli t-shirts.

And Steve Jobs was notorious at Apple for his black turtlenecks, jeans, and New Balance sneakers.

Wear the same thing each day, and you don't have to focus much energy on your attire. (Just make sure you have enough clean clothes!)

---

[16] businessinsider.com/successful-people-like-barack-obama-wear-the-same-thing-every-day-2018-2

Mark Zuckerberg doesn't spend an hour staring at the shirts in his closet every morning, contemplating whether to put on a white or a blue t-shirt. Dr. Dre doesn't waste precious time sorting through his shoe collection.

Financially speaking, we can reduce the decisions we have to make by way of intermittent spending. With intermittent spending, we don't have to put ourselves through the stress of deciding whether or not to spend money—we simply avoid spending money outside of our Spending Window™! If, for example, we commit to avoid spending between 11 a.m. and 3 p.m. on weekdays, we don't have to think about whether we're going to spend during those times. We just don't do it. That's one less decision we're forced to make.

So really, the goal of an intermittent spending program is to become more mindful. Rather than just telling you to be mindful of your spending, this book provides a formula—a plan, or a roadmap—for making good headway. The concept of intermittent spending uses many of the same ideas that have been successful for weight loss in intermittent fasting. Much like a doctor would customize your health plan, you might work with someone—your peers, your family, or even your financial advisor—to customize your own intermittent spending plan.

Your Intermittent Spending Journey Starts Here
This book will put you on the path to start your own personalized intermittent spending regimen.

Not sure where to begin? Well, I'm going to teach you what to do. I'm going to share with you the experiences I've had with others who have turned to intermittent spending and realized success. I'm also going to describe some of the pitfalls of intermittent spending—some of the mines out there that may try to derail you from achieving your goals.

Together, though, we're going to simplify the way you spend money by restricting *when* you spend. We're going to help get you on track.

Really, I don't know that there are any drawbacks to being more mindful about your spending. We live in a society where consumerism is the norm. Socioeconomically speaking, the United States is built on this foundation of increasing consumption of goods and services. Spending more is encouraged, and we haven't really taken the time to look at that.

The Spending Window may well be the solution.

So, what are you waiting for? Let's move on and customize an intermittent spending plan made just for you. Chapter Three will provide an outline you can use to create your own Spending Window™.

Chapter Three
The Spending Window™
Creating Your Custom Plan

Now let's take a deep dive into time-restricted spending.

We'll discuss how to go about creating a Spending Window™, and review the different shapes and styles you can choose from. (Note that these shapes and styles are just some examples of what your personal Spending Window™ might look like.)

Are you ready? Great. Sit back, relax, and prepare to embark on a path of mindful intermittent spending.

Introduction to the Spending Window™
There are a number of books you can read about budgeting, or about what you should and shouldn't do with your money. This isn't one of them. Rather, this book explores mindful spending as a result of creating a designated window.

What's that, you ask? Your Spending Window™ is the timeframe during which you're allowed to spend money. It plays a key role in intermittent or time-restricted spending.

Before we explore this concept further, let's take a step back. Let's go back to intermittent *fasting* for a moment.

Remember that the focus of intermittent fasting is on *when* you ingest food and not necessarily on *what* you ingest.

Intermittent spending works the same way. <u>Again, the focus is on *when*, not *what*.</u>

It doesn't matter whether you're spending your hard-earned cash on food or gas or birthday presents for your kids' friends. What matters is that you only swipe your card or pay cash during your Spending Window™—or the timeframe you've created during which you're able to spend your money.

We've seen the positive effects intermittent fasting can have on your eating habits. When you adopt our program, keep in mind that the same benefits apply to your spending habits.

Why Create a Spending Window™?
In previous chapters, we talked about what's going on in society and why people should focus on their spending habits. Now we're going to shed some light on the importance of creating a Spending Window™.

Here are some reasons for doing so:

1. *A Spending Window™ forces a stop, or at least a break, in your spending.*

2. *It encourages more mindful spending. It makes you slow down and think—particularly when you're outside your window.*

Think of it this way: Say you're browsing an online shop or walking past your favorite clothing store. You see a pair of jeans on your screen, or inside the boutique, and you feel the urge to buy them.

It just so happens that you're not in your Spending Window™.

So, what do you do? If you've committed to your Spending Window™, you'll have to wait. And maybe, just maybe, you'll adopt a different view of the situation. That slowdown in the system—that forced break, as we said above—may well make you reevaluate your urge to buy those jeans.

See if those jeans are still as important a few hours later, when you're within your Spending Window™.

See if you still want to spend money on something you might not need.

If you still want those jeans, then by all means, buy them. Regardless of how you feel, though, having a Spending Window™ will make you think carefully about your decision.

It'll push you not to spend in the moment—unless that moment falls within your window.

The result? The impulse spending will likely decrease. You may even naturally begin to prioritize what matters most to you.

Now, those jeans might not be front and center on your list of priorities. And this brings us to another benefit of adhering to your window. Intermittent spending can help minimize the decision fatigue far too many of us face. You could be bombarded with things to buy, and yet, you may tune most of those things out because they're not in your window.

So, during your window, you'll become more focused. I've seen clients become their best selves, from a financial standpoint, when they're in their Spending Window™.

Becoming Mindful of Your Spending Habits
Periodically, I'll revisit the concept of mindfulness.

As you know, mindfulness is one of the main factors at play in intermittent spending. The benefits of mindful thinking range from healthier eating to relief from anxiety, and from higher productivity to helping you connect more deeply with friends and colleagues.

Spending is no different. When you become more mindful of your spending habits, you'll become more aware of what you typically spend your money on. You'll also grow more in tune with some of the pitfalls that may cause you to stray from your budget.

This is because a Spending Window™ pushes us to prioritize how we spend our money. And creating a window is much easier than building a budget. By creating a Spending Window™ where you can spend funds on whatever you want, you'll feel less restricted. You'll know that you can still indulge in many of the things you enjoy, if only you wait until you're inside your window. Because of this, you'll be more apt to follow your own rules.

It really is a lot like eating. If you eliminate specific foods from your diet, or if you tell yourself you can only consume so many calories each day, you may feel as though you're limiting yourself. Imposing such limits is usually more challenging than saying you can only eat during a specific timeframe or window.

Granted, it does make sense to watch what you're ingesting. There's a reason for the saying "you are what you eat."

Spending is similar. And no, you don't want to spend money on ridiculous items—but denying yourself of all the things you want to buy isn't an ideal solution. A healthy solution would be to start building your Spending Window™. This will allow you to work on what you're spending your hard-earned cash on later down the road.

An added bonus: Your spending window is easy to control. It's easy to digest, and it's easy to adhere to. What's more, since it's completely time-based, there isn't really much to stress about. This is in large part because you do all your thinking and planning in advance. And while yes, there will be challenges—and no, you might not do things perfectly the first time around—it will guide you toward more empowering financial decisions.

Better Spending Habits, Better Life Habits
I want you to think about why you're reading this book.

You want to change your spending habits, right? You want to develop some tactics that can benefit not only your spending, but your life in general?

Think of it this way: Maybe you'll go to the park instead of spending money on a movie, because the showtime isn't inside your Spending Window™. Maybe you'll check out a book from the library instead of buying a hardcover for the same reason.

Decisions like these are obviously going to help you out monetarily in the long run. They're also going to push you to spend more time directly engaged with your family (in the case of the park) and benefiting from your local library (in the case of a book).

The money-saving benefits are just an added bonus.

Chances are you'll stop mindlessly swiping your credit card as a result.

You may start regifting more often or bartering with people.

Instead of paying people for their services, you might offer to do something for them if they do something for you. Who's to say you can't offer free landscaping in exchange for occasional access to your good friend's boat?

By trading with people, you can still adhere to your window. Since your Spending Window™ is about money, there's no need to place limits on your time, or on your emotional bandwidth.

The end goal of this process is to create a long-term trajectory of mindful spending. And these mindful spending habits are easily attainable. Regardless of whether it takes you three weeks or three months to implement your new lifestyle, it really isn't a very long time in the grand scheme of things.

So, now we're going to talk about *your* Spending Window™. I'm going to outline some starter plans, and we'll look into what window is best based on your needs and expectations. You'll have your own personalized framework up and running in no time.

Because just as bad habits are hard to break, good habits are often in it for the long haul too.

A Word on Retirement

The retirement planner in me can't get past this point without mentioning that some of the money you save as a result of your Spending Window™ can easily be redirected to your retirement account! Like all good habits, this will make your life easier down the road.

How to Create Your Spending Window™

How should you design your Spending Window™? What is the best format?

The truth is that there is no ideal format. Everyone's situation is unique. There is not a one-size-fits-all Spending Window™.

Now, if I say you're going to stick to a specific spending plan, during a specific time each day, for eternity—well, chances are you'll fail. You might stick to the plan for a few weeks, but eventually the train's going to go off the tracks, so to speak.

This is why it's important that you customize your window. That you create the window that's best for you and go from there.

Your Spending Window™ should be a part of your natural rhythm. It shouldn't be totally off the chart, nor should it be extremely difficult to manage. For instance, you can't only make your window open while you're sleeping to try and beat the system. That just won't work.

It's like choosing the right food diet. You like the Mediterranean diet? Go for it! Are you more of an Atkins diet fan? No problem. You're not going to love everything about your diet all the time. But you've got to at least not hate it, right?

So, choose the diet—or create the Spending Window™—that works for you. And then, before you know it, you'll see the gains. The improvements. You may even find you enjoy them.

You might also want to consult with a professional before you do anything too drastic.

You could create a plan on your own, and you'll be just fine. A professional, however, might be quite useful when it comes time to focus on what you're spending your money on as opposed to when. A financial professional with expertise in this area could help you—in addition to creating your window—come up with some tactics, or strategies, for staying on track.

But let's talk about the window itself in more detail. People often come to me and say, "Oh, a Spending Window™ is just going to defer my usual spending."

They assume they'll end up spending the same amount when their window's open that they would otherwise, and that intermittent spending is a fruitless effort.

I'd like to let you in on a little something here: These are the naysayers talking. These are the people who say you should just let your kids eat as much junk food and drink as much soda as they want, because if you don't, they'll simply go to college and make up for lost time.

With your Spending Window™, however, I think you'll quickly realize that you're *not* in fact spending the same amount you would under normal circumstances.

Sure, there are going to be certain things you need to spend money on. That's life. That's just how we are, and that isn't a bad thing. The frivolous stuff, on the other hand? The emotional purchases? The needless spending? These are the areas where you're going to see a difference. So, try it before you knock it.

Customizing Your Spending Window™
I want to introduce you to all the different types of Spending Windows™ you have at your disposal. I'd like to show you some different window sizes—the different lengths and timeframes.

You have plenty of options. In the intermittent fasting world, for example, there's a window where you fast for 16 hours and then eat during an eight-hour timeframe. Other dieters might adhere to one meal a day. Some people will fast every other day, and others may stick with their fasting window on and off every other week.

Similar could be said about intermittent spending. I'm going to highlight some templates you can use to customize your Spending Window™.

"the 16:8" Spending Window™

In the 16:8, your Spending Window™ consists of eight hours. This means there are 16 hours of the day when you don't spend money, and then eight hours when you are allowed to spend.

The 16:8 is a fairly accommodating window that you can customize based on your preferred time of day. You might customize your Spending Window™ to include the afternoon and early evening. You might make sure it goes well into nighttime. Or, your 16:8 window could include the morning and part of the midday.

I would recommend that you plan your window in a way that's conducive to being more mindful. Yes, you could have a solid eight-hour Spending Window™—but if that window covers the times you typically spend money, you won't necessarily become more aware of what you're doing. To encourage mindfulness, **consider having half of your window overlap with your workday.** This will help you tighten it—and your spending habits—without completely sacrificing your ability to spend over eight hours each day.

Of course, this is just a recommendation. And above all else, the thing to remember is this: For 16 hours of the day, you're not spending money. Then, for eight hours of the day, you *can* spend money.

"the weekender" Spending Window™

You could commit to an eight-hour Spending Window™ each and every day. Or, you could become a "weekender."

Weekenders may only spend on weekends. Conversely, they might not spend at all on weekends.

The key factor here is to evaluate what's conducive to your lifestyle before committing to a window. If, for instance, going out to dinner is part of your Friday night routine, you should ensure Friday evening falls inside your Spending Window™.

Many people, when they go down this route, will lean more toward spending on the weekends because that's when they have the most social commitments.

Others may find they tend to overspend on weekends. To address this, they might eliminate weekends from their window. And again, the naysayers will say, "Well, you'll just spend more during the week."

If that's the case, so be it. The important thing is that you become more aware of your spending habits. Because that's the whole point of intermittent spending: building awareness during this process.

What you must do is sit down in the beginning and look at yourself. Think about when you tend to spend money, when you tend to make impulse purchases, and when you *need* to spend money. Then, consider when you're in a state to spend money in a really thoughtful way. That's how you'll find the plan that's most sustainable.

"the every-other-day" Spending Window™

I believe there are advantages to all the Spending Window™ formats I'm sharing with you. The every-other-day template, however, is one of my favorites. With this strategy you choose to spend on only certain days of the week.

Why is this one of my favorites?

Because you're forced to eliminate those daily spending habits you might not be aware of. Whether you commit to a Monday-Wednesday-Friday-Sunday window or a Tuesday-Thursday-Saturday Spending Window™, you'll learn to become significantly more mindful than you were before you began this process. You'll stop going out to lunch on a daily basis, and you'll forego your morning latte certain days of the week.

And maybe you'll cheat. When you do a full day of "spending fasting," as I like to call it, you may end up asking a friend to buy you a cup of coffee. (Be sure to cover them the next time if you make this ask.) But overall, you'll become more aware of your spending. And that's what's most vital.

"the extended" **Spending Window™.**

Not quite ready to jump headfirst into a long-term Spending Window™?

No problem. Though it depends on the person, some might do well to start with an extended window. To dip your toes into the world of intermittent spending, you might take on a short-term "no-spend challenge."

How does this work? You could forego spending for a weekend, or a holiday weekend, or even a full week if you're able to plan your expenses around it. If you like what you see, or if you want to continue experimenting, you could plan an extended Spending Window™ into your schedule each month.

I believe this is a great way to get involved with intermittent spending. It isn't for everyone, but for some people, an extended window is easier because there are no questions about what the window is. A rule is a rule—and if you're not going to spend for an entire-seven-day period, you'll have a great understanding of the boundaries you've set for yourself. This will force you to be quite thoughtful in your approach.

A word for the wise, though: If you're going down this path, be sure to do some planning ahead of time. Then, you can easily reintroduce your spending in a controlled fashion, at which point you'll be aware of when you can and cannot spend.

In this way, an extended Spending Window™ will help you get over those hunger pangs you may experience at the beginning of your "fast." Think of it like a detox program.

Pick A Window That Works For You

No matter the window you choose, you'll become much more aware of your spending habits. You'll likely make changes for the better. And chances are you'll have a clear grasp of what you truly need to spend your money on, and what is simply frivolous or luxury.

the 16:8	Window open for 8 consecutive hours per day	
the weekender	Window open only on weekends. Could also be reversed and window open only during the week.	
the every-other-day	Window open all day, every-other-day.	
the extended	Window closed for 3+ consecutive days. May be a week long, month long, or year long spending fast!	

Uncharted Waters: Automatic Payments
Let's discuss automatic payments.

We're talking utilities, mortgage or rent payments, and expenses like car or health insurance. You may have these payments set up automatically. At the very least, they're necessary—you can't just skip making them.

So, how should you handle these expenses in the context of your Spending Window™?

Here's the deal: Regardless of how you've structured your window, there are going to be certain purchases that just come up. There are going to be certain expenses that you simply can't go without.

And with automatic payments, in particular, there's going to be a specific day of the month—and likely even a set time—that the funds will be deducted from your card or bank account. You can't necessarily control the logistics, nor are you necessarily aware of them.

What should you do in these cases?

Maybe you set up your window to start before a deduction is made. Maybe you do it immediately after a deduction is made. This is a slippery slope, and there's no right answer. The crucial thing is to know what those fixed payments are—and to try to work them into your Spending Window™ to the best of your abilities.

Including these payments in your Spending Window™ forces you to factor them in. That way, when you look at your spending, these payments are right there in front of you. They're not just some nebulous thing you don't even think about.

And who knows? You might even identify some recurring payments you weren't aware of—some subscriptions you no longer want or need. Being mindful of these scheduled payments will help you become more intentional in your spending.

With that, I urge you to review your automatic payments and build your Spending Window™ around them—or vice versa. But take the time to look at your recurring expenses. You'll build better habits as a result.

Holding Yourself Accountable
For some of us, accounting is easy. We know exactly what money is coming into our accounts, and we know what money is going out.

Other people might not have as solid a grasp on their finances. Some people might not think about the little things. Planning for the unexpected might be a bit more difficult.

This is where we can simplify our finances. It's important to measure your spending, in this way, because if you don't account for it, there's no way to control it. You've got to start by going over some of your fixed expenses.

Why don't you review them right now? Grab a piece of paper and a pen or open a Word document on your computer. Then, for each fixed expense, ask yourself questions such as:

- *How much is this expense?*
- *How often will this payment come out of my account?*

- *Is this payment actually necessary?*

Take as much time as you need to answer these questions. From there, you can build your Spending Window™ around your responses.

Does this make sense? Good. I also want you to keep in mind that some of your expenses are actually very positive. Putting aside money for retirement—your 401k and your IRA, for instance—is a solid practice. These payments typically come right out of your paycheck and go toward your future.

As a financial planner, I'm never going to tell you to ignore your retirement. Quite the opposite. But I want you to be aware of exactly how much money you're contributing to your future. Some people don't even know how much they're putting away! They might take a closer look at things and realize, *Oh, I need to beef up my contribution.* Or, *Oh, I could pause my subscription to one of the four online services I'm paying for and move that money toward my retirement.*

From here, the outflow is the same—but it's much better. You won't be able to benefit financially, though, until you realize exactly what you're spending your money on. And I think that having a window and forcing yourself to actually schedule your expenses inside that window, can be a valuable exercise.

Nothing is permanent. And being more mindful of your spending will reinforce the fact that impermanence is the rule. So, remember that your intermittent spending experience is a journey, not a sprint. Remember that you're going to need to modify your plan over time and make adjustments to your window—and life's going to throw you curveballs here and there.

But one thing I want to reiterate is that you have to factor your support network into your plan. You have to include your friends and family. I don't necessarily mean you have to tell your coworkers about your finances, or even about what you're doing. I do, however, want you to factor in how you're going to handle these situations.

Put simply, you have to think about you. You need to examine what you're going to do based on what feels right to you.

Does your office go out for happy hour every Thursday? To avoid ostracizing yourself from your colleagues, make sure your window includes that.

Is your family planning a vacation? Great. Make sure your Spending Window™ accounts for everything you need to purchase leading up to your big trip. You have to think about these things, and you have to allow for these scenarios.

Then, with a little preplanning, you'll have no problem. And additionally, you'll be surprised by how supportive your inner circle will be. Your loved ones may even help you overcome the challenges you face as you navigate your Spending Window™.

Just as you're building new habits, you're also building a support network. Because the truth is that it's easier if you let others know what you're doing. You might just say, "This is what I'm doing," and then leave it at that. Or you could tell your friends that intermittent spending is a personal challenge and they'll probably respect you more for it.

What About Cash?
Before I end this chapter, I want to bring up the role cash plays in the context of a Spending Window™. Though some would argue it's best to avoid spending outside your window altogether, others will tell you cash is the exception.

One idea I've seen successfully implemented is a ***cash allowance***. A person might create their window, and within that timeframe they'll reserve up to, say, $40 per week for luxury items, emergency expenses, or even treats for their children. This practice is a bit nuanced, but it's been done. It's kind of like including a "cheat day" in your diet plan.

The idea here is that you're still forcing mindfulness. You're planning for the week. And if this means you get to enjoy your daily coffee without swiping your credit card, then that's just as well.

Again, it's a slippery slope. I do think having cash on hand forces people to be mindful, and that an allowance can keep you from going overboard—but you shouldn't use cash as a tool to consistently spend outside your window.

I've said it once, and I'll say it again: You need to remember the reason you've created your Spending Window™. You need to understand *why* you're committing to a lifestyle of intermittent spending. Think about these things, and watch your decision evolve into long-term financial stability. No matter what your window looks like—no matter what you include in it, and no matter what you leave out—you'll be poised to transform your spending habits for the better.

Does this make sense? If so, let's move on and discuss how you can measure your intermittent spending progress.

Chapter Four
Measuring Progress
Evaluating Your Spending Window™

It's easy, isn't it? Anyone can create a Spending Window™.

Now that you've created yours, the rest of your intermittent-spending journey should be relatively simple. The question now is how to go about tracking your progress. How can you be sure you're taking the proper steps?

This chapter will explore some of the steps you can take to stay on track.

Starting Small for Successful Time-Restricted Spending
Though it's important to consider the big picture, it's vital to start small when you create your Spending Window™.

You can always work your way up to a more complex framework. In the early stages, however, you should aim to work out a system where you can be ***disciplined.***

Let's go back to our food analogy. You know how some diets include what are known as cheat days? I, personally, don't love the concept of a cheat day—a day where you can eat anything you like, even if it's in direct contradiction with your food plan—because it gives people an excuse to avoid being disciplined.

So, forgive yourself if you slip up when adhering to your Spending Window™—but don't cheat. Instead, start small to make lasting changes, and work hard to maintain that sense of discipline. Even if you refrain from spending just one day each week, you'll be well on your way to success.

What Are You Hoping to Achieve with Your Spending Window™?

We've talked about tailoring your window to your lifestyle. Now we're going to discuss making sure it's well-suited to your goals.

So, ask yourself what exactly you are hoping to achieve. One of the best ways to change your financial behavior, I've found, is to accept the fact that you aren't happy with the way things are going now.

But what specifically are you hoping to change? What is it about your financial life that you want to improve? Take a moment to consider those questions, and then commit to your Spending Window™. Changing your spending is not easy, but in my opinion, it is the most direct way to fix your financial problems.

This is where those *measurable goals* come in. Just like diet is very much a numbers game—you need to manage your caloric intake, and you need the right quantities of macronutrients to ensure success—so too is spending.

So, what are your measurable spending goals?

Maybe you want to reduce your spending by $200 per week.

Maybe you hope to save an additional $1,000 each month.

Maybe you'd like to set a tangible daily budget.

Think about what it is you want to accomplish. Take a minute or two right now and jot those goals down below or on a separate piece of paper.

Measurable Financial Goal #1

_____
_____
_____
_____
_____

Measurable Financial Goal #2

_____
_____
_____
_____
_____

Measurable Financial Goal #3

_____
_____
_____
_____
_____

Have you finished writing down your goals? Great. The next step is to determine whether your Spending Window™ is conducive to achieving them. You can do this by measuring whether you're able to adhere to your intermittent spending plan.

Are you getting through your window without cheating—without making frequent mistakes? If staying inside your window is a struggle, you may want to reevaluate the structural decisions you've made.

And again, this is why your goals are so important. Granular, thoughtful goals—a key component of any leadership program, I've found—will let you know whether you're on the right track.

Reviewing Your Credit Card and Bank Statements
This chapter is all about measuring your progress as you dive deeper into your intermittent spending experience. A simple but often overlooked way of tracking success is to review your credit card and bank statements.

Say, for example, that you spend everything on a credit card. If you make all your payments by credit card, at the end of the month you'll have full access to a statement that provides a clear picture of your spending. You'll be able to see the exact dates and even, quite possibly, the times you made each purchase.

The same thing applies to your bank statements. You can review these documents at the end of the month to track your financial progress and assess whether you are following your Spending Window™. Bank statements also present a great opportunity to identify things you might not even know you're spending money on.

If you haven't watched a show on HBO in months, for instance, it might be time to cancel that subscription—something you may not even be conscious of.

Pro-tip: Regardless of how detailed your credit card statements are, you should get in the habit of tracking all your spending. To do this, start keeping a journal or a folder of all your receipts. While debit card transactions are almost always instantly recorded and seen on bank apps, you'll want to have all those dates, times, and purchase amounts on hand—no matter your approach.

With that, I urge you to measure your progress. To ensure your success in our program by tracking your spending both inside and outside your window. Because if you don't measure your spending, you won't manage it. And if you don't manage it, intermittent spending—the very concept of a Spending Window™—won't help you.

A Word on Cash and Apps
How much cash do you use outside your Spending Window™?

In Chapter 3, we discussed the possibility of including a cash allowance in your window. This is all well and good, but you want to make sure you measure how much cash you spend outside your window. This shouldn't be a common occurrence, but the most important thing is to be aware of your spending behavior. So, if you spend cash—within but more importantly outside your window—write it down.

If you don't document your spending, then you might not succeed on your intermittent spending journey. And speaking of success, it's important to be mindful of *all* your spending habits.

We've talked about credit cards, we've talked about cash, and now we're going to talk about online purchases and apps like Amazon and Postmates. Apps make it extremely easy to spend money on pretty much everything you can imagine: books, movies, clothes, takeout, you name it. Though it may seem like you can buy whatever you want, whenever you want, that doesn't mean you *should* make every impulse purchase that beckons to you.

How can you address this? A great strategy here is to place all the apps that may entice you to spend money in a designated folder on your phone or on your desktop. You can then make a conscious decision to only visit those apps when you're inside your Spending Window™. Work to build new and empowering habits, and soon you'll be curating a more successful financial life.

Eliminating Impulse Spending
What is the problem with the apps we mentioned above? They're highly conducive to impulse spending.

A core goal, in creating your Spending Window™, is to eliminate impulse spending altogether.

You see, impulse spending is arguably one of the main drivers of people's financial problems. So, if you can use the concept of a Spending Window™ to purge those impulses, you're already making sound progress. Though you may still want to spend during your window, the window itself will make you more mindful of the purchases you hope to make.

At the very least, you'll take the time to consider that new gadget or that delicious bakery cake before you swipe your card. And you'll be more mindful when you're outside your window.

Let's relate this back to intermittent fasting for a moment. If a person is halfway through an 18-hour fast, and they want to eat a mint or enjoy a cocktail, they are still—even if they are only indulging in something small—breaking their fast. Physically, the second they start eating again, they are changing their physiology.

Your Spending Window™ is no different. If you want to buy a small coffee from time to time, or if you notice a killer sale on a day outside of your window—you are still cheating.

The process is meant to be black-and-white. There's no gray area (not much of one, anyway), and therefore, there's little room for error. At the beginning of your journey, to mitigate those impulse purchases, you'll want to analyze the spending you do both inside and outside your window.

Successful Spending Outcomes: Money In, Money Out
Why did you create your Spending Window™?

We've talked about setting measurable goals. Now let's talk about why you decided to commit to a Spending Window™in the first place.

Were you spiraling into debt? Were you grappling with a negative balance every month, and looking for a way to stop the bleeding? Were you simply trying to get your financial situation under control?

An easy strategy for measuring whether the bleeding has stopped, so to speak, is to look for a net-positive in your cash flow. In this way, you may want to use a *cash flow statement* to ensure successful spending outcomes.

It's simple, really: a cash flow statement is the money you have coming in compared to the money you have going out.

While reviewing your cash flow statement, you'll want to look at your income. You'll want to examine the money you spend as well, and you'll want to be at a zero balance at the very least—ideally a positive balance.

Some people, however, don't even know whether their balance is positive or negative. They just go through their lives—and their spending—mindlessly, taking whatever outcome is presented to them.

Has Your Spending Behavior Changed?
Have you truly changed your spending behavior?

Here is an indicator that might help you answer that question. It's not going to be data-driven, necessarily—it might be more anecdotal—but this is something you'll want to watch for as you evaluate your Spending Window™.

The indicator is this: You may start to question your purchases. Like I said, most people go through life without really thinking about what they're buying. They might say they'll shop for the best price, but they'll rarely stop and ask themselves, *Why am I buying this to begin with?*

And yet, once you start asking yourself whether your purchases make sense—whether they represent a need or a want—then that's another indicator. And if you start categorizing things as either wants or needs, then you can make more mindful decisions as you navigate the intermittent spending process.

That's what it's all about: mindful spending.

Consider a 30-Day Trial Period
To properly evaluate the metrics involved in intermittent spending, I recommend a trial period of four weeks or 30 days. This will allow you to evaluate your spending in a convenient, comfortable way. Remember how Kim and Joe did this in our Introduction?

So, for one month, consider sitting down each week to track your progress. A reminder that you'll want to consider the following factors:

- Your cash spending, both inside and outside your window
- Your credit card spending, both inside and outside your window
- All your online shopping, both inside and outside your window

Throughout this process, you'll want to *analyze, analyze, analyze.* You'll want to pay close attention to what you're spending money on (and when).

Say, for example, a furniture expense comes up. One day you wake up, and you decide it's time to invest in a new kitchen table, or a new recliner for your living room.

The purchase, ideally, should be something you think about inside your Spending Window™. Inside your window, you are a little more focused and a little less distracted—a little more mindful and a little less emotional in your decision-making.

This again is where that trial period comes in. For all major purchases like our furniture example above, you should reflect on whether you are waiting until you are inside your Spending Window™ to make a decision. If you find time and again that you are financing these purchases outside your window, you may want to—at the end of your month-long trial—adjust the timeframe to better accommodate your lifestyle.

Say you walk by an appealing high-end gym on your way to work every morning. If you find yourself constantly tempted to invest in a three-year membership, but your Spending Window™ only allows you to swipe your card on weekends, you should wait to consider whether you really need that membership.

Then, if after a month goes by you still want to walk in and swipe your card, you can adjust your Spending Window™ to accommodate that. This will help to measure your behavior and structure your window in a way that's effective and challenging in equal measure.

Emphasis on Results
We've talked about measuring behavior—but what about measuring outcomes? You'll want to take a look at the actual results of your Spending Window™ to see how effective it is. At the end of every week, or at the end of every month, you'll want to contemplate the changes taking place with your bank and credit card statements.

Be consistent for 30 days and see what happens. Determine at that point whether you're sneaking outside your window and funding impulse purchases. See then whether you've created the best-fitting window for your needs.

This is the time to make adjustments and become a little more restrictive if you aren't seeing the results you want. Consider the following outcomes as you pivot your Spending Window™:

- You have more cash at the end of the month than you did when you started.
- Your cash flow is becoming positive.
- You are zeroing balance.

- You are adding to your bank account instead of taking away from it.

Odds are that if you stick to your window, you're going to increase the funds in your bank account. More importantly, odds are that you will become significantly more mindful of the way you spend your money. Maybe, if you're a techie, you'll realize you don't actually need the latest and greatest phone or computer or gadget.

Maybe you'll learn you don't actually need to buy those new shoes. Maybe, like in our gym example earlier in the chapter, you'll have a gut feeling that you don't actually *need* a three-year membership, and you'll complete a free 14-day workout trial before taking the plunge (or deciding to stick with your home gym).

Small changes like this are in fact our biggest success stories. They may sound small, but mindfulness really is the end result. The ultimate goal is to eliminate the desire to spend impulsively, or the craving to spend money on things you don't really need.

Spending enlightenment will follow. It's well within reach.

Chapter Five
COVID-19
Spending Habits During a Global Pandemic

This book began to take shape in the early stages of the COVID-19 pandemic.

With stay-at-home orders spanning the nation, and 10.5 million confirmed coronavirus cases here in the U.S. as of the writing of this book on November 12, 2020, our collective outlook has shifted. Our daily routines look very different than they did a year ago. Some of our financial habits have changed as well.

An Unexpected Path Toward Intermittent Spending
There's no question the COVID-19 crisis has been a net-negative on society. With jobs lost and lives in jeopardy, I don't want to imply the coronavirus is a good thing.

I do think, however, that there's a silver lining in every cloud. I'll go on to say that not all the changes resulting from the coronavirus are bad, per se. There may even be some financial takeaways from this experience that we'll carry with us for the rest of our lives.

I think that if we take a step back and look at intermittent spending unemotionally, the pandemic may well have presented a valuable financial opportunity.

Let me begin by saying that one of the things I see in my profession is not enough saving for retirement. We've discussed the importance of personal saving. There's no question that saving money is highly beneficial.

So, in terms of the rate at which we save, what can we learn from the coronavirus pandemic?

Let's consider some valuable data from the **Federal Reserve Bank of St. Louis**.[17] The bank publishes Americans' personal saving rate each month. In this chapter, we're going to examine the timeframe from January through June 2020.

Personal Savings in the U.S. in the First Half of 2020

Month (2020)	Personal Savings Rate (%)	Difference from the Previous Month (%)
January	7.6	-
February	8.3	9.2
March	12.8	54.2
April	33.5	161.7
May	24.2	-27.8
June	19.0	-21.5

You'll notice a pretty substantial jump from March to April 2020. It may seem counterintuitive, but as the pandemic became more serious in the U.S., our personal saving rate increased significantly—nearly threefold.

How could that have happened?

Why were people saving so much money?

What shift was taking place during these transformative months?

---

[17] fred.stlouisfed.org/series/PSAVERT

These data are proof that from a financial standpoint, the COVID-19 pandemic *changed* something for people.

Why Did We Start Saving More Money?
In the media during quarantine, we heard a lot about how income was down for people. Some were simply making less money; others were furloughed or laid off altogether.

There was talk of the economy plummeting—going downward. Yet, many people's bank accounts were moving upward.

Sure, this could have been explained at least in part by the stimulus checks, or economic impact payments, the federal government issued.[18] Individuals earning less than $75,000 per year received $1,200 in response to the coronavirus; families with dependents were granted an additional $500 per dependent (up to three).

Government incentive programs may have played a role as well. Grants too. There were also those $600 weekly bonuses in people's unemployment checks due to COVID-19, and then half that amount in the late summer of 2020—bonuses that created situations where some were earning more in unemployment benefits than they were from their pre-coronavirus income.

I believe, however, that there was something more at play. I think we'd being doing everyone a disservice by examining things in a silo.

Just like the data from the Federal Reserve Bank of St. Louis, statistics from the **Bureau of Economic Analysis**

---

[18] irs.gov/coronavirus/economic-impact-payments

were telling.[19] Experts revealed that personal income increased by 10.5% from March to April 2020, and that consumer spending decreased by 13.6% during this same timeframe.

Pre-pandemic, on the other hand? Let's take a look at the following graph:[20]

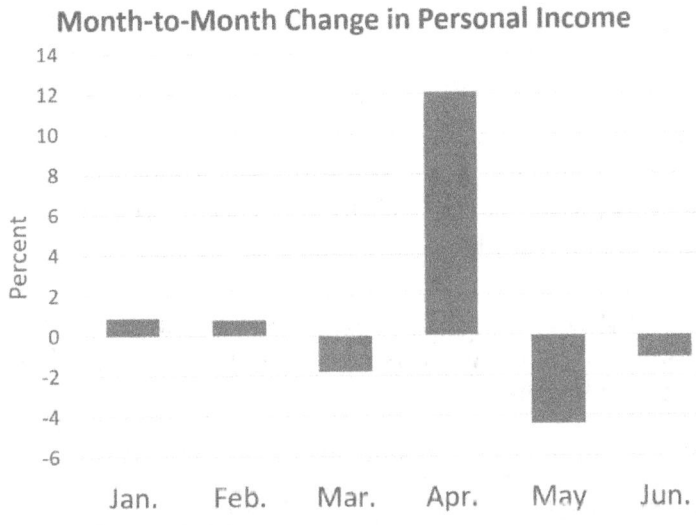

A quick note: These are just monthly estimates of Americans' personal income in the first half of 2020. We don't know the real numbers just yet because not enough time has passed, and there's really a great deal of data to collect.

---

[19] bea.gov/data/income-saving/personal-income
[20] bea.gov/system/files/pi0620.png

What I can say with certainty is that there's a clear trend. That trend is this: Spending went down drastically. The reasons for this are obvious. We'll discuss them as we move through this chapter.

Coronavirus Spending Habits: Lasting Changes Post-Pandemic
The novel coronavirus pandemic not only impacted our health, but it also caused a marked lifestyle shift. With stay-at-home orders in place from coast to coast, and nonessential businesses closed, people weren't spending much money on social situations.

Maybe you got together with friends for FaceTime dates or Zoom meetings during COVID-19.

Maybe you met your loved ones for drinks via video chat and simply filled your glass with whatever you had lying around the house.

Maybe you played Animal Crossing instead of bowling or rock climbing.

These virtual get-togethers were likely less expensive than the in-person events you relied on pre-pandemic. In this way, decreased spending was undeniably a byproduct of the coronavirus.

And now, as we reopen the country, we must ask ourselves: What can we maintain where our spending is concerned? How can we tailor our window to include what we learned during these unprecedented times?

Let's take these questions a step further and examine the areas in which our spending decreased. Some of the industries most affected were the biggest areas of spending for many of us: **dining**, **retail**, and **travel**.

Our spending in these areas did decrease; the data doesn't deny that. The caveat, though, is that people shifted their spending to other areas.

Just as people were meeting their friends online instead of going out with them, people were spending their hard-earned cash online.

So, there is a bit of a wash here.

That said, our impulse buying has gone down significantly now that things have settled.

If you're ordering a meal via food delivery service, you're less likely to tack on dessert at the end of the night.

If you're browsing online retailers instead of walking into a shop, you're less likely to buy that trendy shirt you don't need—because you can't see or feel it.

Impulse purchases were fundamentally put to a standstill after the initial shock of the pandemic—and while this was essentially forced on people, I personally think the behavior will continue moving forward.

I think that looking back years from now, the coronavirus will have transformed our impulsive spending behavior in a fairly significant way.

Travel, Spending, and the Coronavirus

Traveling puts us in a position where spending is going to be forced. And in the spring of 2020, few people weren't traveling for nonessential reasons.

I'm not only talking about recreational travel, like the spring trip you might have been planning before the pandemic took over our lives, but also nonessential workers' daily commutes.

Think of it this way: No matter the nature of your trip, you're probably spending money. Whether you are traveling for a vacation, traveling across state lines to see friends, or traveling for business, *you are probably spending money.*

While focusing on your travel expenses, you might create a Spending Window™ based on what you've learned from the pandemic.

You might ask yourself:

- *How can I modify those travel expenses?*
- *How can I plan financially in a way that will minimize the impact of those travel costs?*

One example that comes to mind is that of a business meeting. Before the pandemic, maybe you had to drive 45 minutes in your car to get to a weekly meeting. You had to spend money on gas, put mileage on your vehicle, and maybe even pick up a coffee on your way.

Post-pandemic, your company or client may well continue to hold meetings online instead of in person. Maybe you're the one who vouches for those virtual meetings. And suddenly, all those expenses disappear.

Suddenly, you don't have to pay for gas. You don't have to put miles on your car, and you can brew a pot of coffee at home.

So maybe, moving forward, we can continue relying on software like Zoom and Microsoft Teams—platforms that became so popular during quarantine—as a way to save time and money.

There's been talk of our "new normal," but only time will tell how things progress. At this point, a spike in mindful behavior would certainly be a good place to start.

Strategies for Improving Our Financial Lives
What habits are most conducive to intermittent spending?

What can people continue to practice, that they picked up during lockdown, to create an effective Spending Window™?

I think that while we can reevaluate our travel and leisure expenditures, there may well be a bounce-back when the pandemic comes to an end. We may find there's a collective pent-up desire for things to go back to the way they were before COVID-19.

Basically, cutting back on nights out with friends, and on family vacations, may be somewhat difficult.

But some things might stick—like cooking more often instead of going out to a restaurant, for instance.

Or, you may get more creative.

Many families, when the pandemic was at its peak, were going stir-crazy from being inside. And with restaurants and movie theaters and playgrounds closed, they had to be resourceful.

As a result, the use of state and local parks skyrocketed. The cost of these parks are a fraction of expensive activities like going to the arcade or the ice rink, or seeing a new release in theaters.

Speaking of movie theaters, another opportunity to save money involves relying on a streaming service. For couples and families, the monthly cost of a streaming service is much less than going to the movies would be. And that's just where the tickets are concerned—not the, some would say, *overpriced* popcorn and candy and drinks.

Moving forward, we'll have to examine whether this is an area where people will continue to want to save. Or, maybe there will there be a pent-up demand to go back to the theater?

No matter the outcome of this unique situation, we'll find out what happens in the months and years that follow. Because again, these experiential elements have shifted. The way we experience the world has shifted. And we have been forced to reexamine our discretionary spending.

What Happens Next?
When it comes to spending money, I think the pandemic was a perfect opportunity for people to try new things.

In large part, this is because people were forced to budget after losing their jobs. I don't want to make light of this, but perhaps we can still catch a glimpse of that silver lining.

Regardless of your pandemic experience, chances are you've been forced to take a look at your spending. Maybe you or a loved one has identified the nonessential items you've been spending your money on, and you are making changes accordingly.

By taking a long, hard look at where your money was going before COVID-19, you can start to examine your discretionary spending in a new and healthy way. Yes, emotions are likely running high—but what a great start kicking off your intermittent spending experience!

That's the point I've wanted to drive home throughout this process. By focusing on intermittent spending, and by having a Spending Window™, I want to emphasize that we are really forcing ourselves to fundamentally *think* before we spend.

Many people are now doing this not because they wanted to, but because they needed to—as a direct result of the global pandemic.

The same thing applies to every adult in the country, if not the world. Everyone has had to think about their income, particularly at the beginning of the crisis, when we didn't know the length or the magnitude of what was going on.

No one knew what was coming.

No one knew the duration, or how long the pandemic was going to last. Remember those first few weeks when people were hoarding toilet paper?

I think that this whole experience came as a surprise to most of us. I also think there's a lot we can learn from it.

A Return to Mindfulness in Lockdown
Starting in the spring of 2020, our nation shut down in many ways.

Some people faced layoffs and furloughs during quarantine. Others had their businesses closed or even boarded up. Even those whose jobs were not at risk—civil servants, teachers, and healthcare practitioners—had to examine their spending.

Did you glance at your wallet? Did you examine your account balances and bank statements at any point during the pandemic?

Chances are that you did. And just thinking about the inflow and outflow of money—and alternatives to our typical spending habits—put many of us in a position of power. In a position of *mindfulness* that we probably wouldn't have been in if it weren't for the global pandemic.

And coincidentally, as the crisis went on, the rioting and business closures due to protests against police brutality and racial discrimination made this period a true lockdown. There were curfews as activists and anarchists clashed. Millions upon millions of Americans grappled with this forced timeout from their normal spending habits.

Now, this isn't to say that everyone took a spending break. We discussed how impulse purchases occurred less frequently during the pandemic, but that wasn't always the case. Nor was it the case for everyone.

Impulse Purchases During the Pandemic
In late April 2020, Credit Karma released an interesting survey about Americans' spending habits.[21] The survey found that 35% of those polled said they had engaged in impulse spending to help manage stress during the coronavirus pandemic.

---

[21] creditkarma.com/insights/i/coronavirus-stress-spending-survey/

Impulse purchases, it's worth noting, are one of the main drivers of poor financial performance.

If you think about the financial negatives of the global pandemic, stress is undeniably a factor. It's also interesting to note that in this survey, 60% of respondents said they were spending either less or a lot less during the pandemic. 18%, however, claimed they were spending more than they did before the virus emerged.

So, while people are spending less overall, those who *are* spending more are doing so in large part due to anxiety and stress. This reveals a relationship between mindfulness and spending—and it may have brought to light an underlying issue we all face.

What About People's Retirement Funds?
If you thought about your retirement during the global pandemic, you may have taken a close look at the Coronavirus Aid, Relief, and Economic Security (CARES) Act.

On March 27, 2020, the CARES Act was signed into law.[22] It's a bit nuanced, but in terms of retirement planning, it allowed people to take an early withdrawal of up to $100,000 from their retirement accounts—without the 10% penalty tax the law imposes on those under the age of 59.5.

It's going to take some time for the data to catch up. We won't know right away how many people took advantage of the law. We must consider, however, the fact that if

---

[22] home.treasury.gov/policy-issues/cares

paychecks went down across the board, then the retirement savings rate went down by default as well.

Yes, people were saving more. Did they apply those savings to their retirement? Probably not.

Anecdotally, given the nature of what I do, I can say a lot of people were putting more of their money in cash in order to deal with lost wages resulting from the pandemic, or to cope with the uncertainty of not knowing what would happen next. COVID-19, in the earliest months, wasn't a time of long-term financial planning because everything was so uncertain.

I will say I saw a lot of people use their stimulus checks to pay off current debts. Others added the money to their rainy-day fund. Both were viable options (and probably savvy).

Lessons Learned About Spending Windows™ from the COVID-19 Experience
There are a couple of things you should think about if you're going to sit down with a pen and paper to devise your window.

First, I want you to focus on being mindful of what you've been spending your money on and when. During the pandemic, I think people had more time to see what was happening—to identify where their money was going.

If, during COVID-19, you realized how much you enjoyed going on family bike rides, you may later on decide to skip that trip to Europe and plan a vacation at a less expensive cycling destination instead.

If, during COVID-19, you realized how much money you were saving by foregoing daily lattes and restaurant dinners, you may want to reflect on how to best approach your discretionary spending post-pandemic.

When it comes to being more mindful, leisure, recreation, and food outside the house are great places to start.

It's worth noting, though, that we can still overspend at the grocery store.

Some people overspent by hoarding food during COVID-19. Some people took up cooking (or, as we all saw on social media, banana bread baking and sourdough making). There was talk of gaining weight from being stuck at home, and of grocery bills spiraling out of control, because the grocery store was one of the few places we could frequent outside the house during the stay-at-home order. In the frenzy of the grocery store, some of us made more impulse purchases.

We even saw this with toilet paper. Talk about impulse spending! People, in a collective panic, were buying toilet paper—along with hand sanitizer and cleansing wipes, canned foods, bread, rice, and pasta—such that these items were flying off the shelves. Emotions were running high in the earliest days of the pandemic, and so too was impulse spending.

So, let's learn from this. Let's investigate how our spending might have increased in areas we didn't think about before the pandemic and examine where it might have decreased.

At this point, this is all we can do. We're still waiting to see how the crisis has impacted our overall spending. Five years from now, looking at a chart of long-term spending, these life-altering months might just be a blip.

What that chart won't show? The thought process behind where some of our spending habits changed. These habits are so important; we must pay attention to them to truly learn from them.

Here's one takeaway: The more control you have over your Spending Window™, the better off you'll be.

A Greater Focus on Social Interactions

Everyone has had their own experience with the pandemic. Most of us, though, have taken the time to better understand ourselves.

I think another one of the financial lessons we can all learn from this time is that our social outings are in fact worthwhile (for the most part). We've now experienced how difficult it can be to not have that in-person social interaction—and moving forward, more and more people will recognize how valuable it really is.

Social excursions are something most people need to make sure they keep in their Spending Window™—even if that spending is discretionary, or nonessential.

It's like dieting, really. If you eliminate all the foods you love, you'll end up unhappy. The same thing applies to our social lives.

With that, I urge you to factor some leeway into your window—some areas where you can engage in social spending scenarios to avoid common mental health concerns.

It's all about being content in our lives. We can't discount that. Even those who previously discounted the benefits of dinners and get-togethers may now see that social gatherings can be very meaningful.

Spending Takeaways from the COVID-19 Pandemic
2020 came, and a global pandemic caught us by surprise.

Financially speaking, many of us were forced to tighten the belt.

We were forced to analyze our spending habits.

Stores only being open for certain hours of the day forced people to shop at certain times.

The closure of hair salons and gyms forced people to maintain their grooming and fitness regimens in other ways—and perhaps rethink their spending. (How many of you started coloring your hair in the bathroom sink? How many of you began exercising at home?)

Leaks in the buckets were plugged. Subscriptions and other expenses that had long gone unused were brought to light. Finally, we had time to really take the time to *think*.

That gym membership you never used, or the monthly payments you've been making to HBO, or the *Wall Street Journal* subscription you got for your birthday and then promptly forgot about—now you know. And you can either start using these items again, or you can cancel the monthly payments and move forward.

At the writing of this book, we don't know what the future will bring. We do know the coronavirus pandemic has presented a great opportunity for people to learn and experiment with different forms of intermittent spending.

And now, as restrictions lift, we can continue to be mindful of where we spend our money—and when.

That's the big question, isn't it?

The big question is whether people are going to be more mindful of their spending. Whether we're going to be financially prepared for the next global event.

Few people actually predicted what a profound impact the coronavirus would have on our society. And I don't want to take on an overly pessimistic outlook, but I guarantee that something else will come up over the course of our lives. Something we're not even aware of yet.

Just as people are going to make sure they have a few extra rolls of toilet paper on hand from here on out, people may inherently become more aware of their spending habits. Because the more we take on a financial maintenance state—a state of financial preparedness—the better equipped we'll be to handle the unexpected.

Why not create a Spending Window™ now to mitigate that future risk? By doing so, you can build good financial habits that will stick with you for the long term.

Chapter Six
Sticky Money
Spending for the Long Term

Let's discuss "sticky money"—a term that involves sticking around for the long haul, financially speaking.

The Spending Window™ is meant to be a long-term habit. It's designed to be a lifestyle, if you will. In this chapter, we'll talk about why that's important. We'll talk about how intermittent spending improves people's lives, gets them away from poor habits, and brings them closer to long-term financial success.

We'll also talk about how the Spending Window™ may help you incrementally fix the financial leaks, so to speak, in your savings. And we'll discuss how, if you start early with your window, you can substantially grow your savings over time.

The Cracked Pot: A Financial Parable
What better way than an analogy to illustrate the importance of building and adhering to your Spending Window™? I'm going to share two of them with you—one at the beginning of this chapter, and one at the end. We'll start with a parable known as *The Cracked Pot*.

A brief summary: Picture someone transporting two full pots of water down a path.

The caveat? One of the pots is cracked. And by the time the person reaches their destination, the cracked pot has less water in it than the other. It's only half-full.

At first the person hauling the water might think the cracked pot is defective in some way. They might think the leak is bad because the pot can't hold as much water.

This, however, isn't inherently true. Back on the path, the person may realize there are flowers growing where they were previously holding the cracked pot. Maybe the cracked pot was helping to water the plants in the surrounding area, creating new life and adding an entirely different kind of value.

The idea is that even the most visible flaws can be beneficial. They can teach us things, they can bring us closer to our goals, and often it's all about cause and effect, just like it was with the flowers and the cracked pot.

You might look at the pots in the parable as pools of money—as your savings—and find that some of your own personal funds will fall out of your cracked pot from time to time, as you walk along your own path.

The objective here is to fill the holes in your finances. Easy, right? You simply plug the leaks and move forward.

The truth, however, is that just like dieting, it can be very difficult to stop up all the leaks in your budget. Managing your finances is above all else a process, and while it's important to be mindful, there must be room for error. This is where your cracked pot comes in.

Manage the Leaks in Your Window
A leak is an unplanned expenditure. Sometimes you are going to have a money outflow that wasn't part of the original plan. This is okay. We can't patch every leak in our Spending Window™.

What we can do is aim to *manage* the leaks in our window (or in our proverbial cracked pot). In some cases, to make sure our habits truly stick, we might even purposefully create leaks—or patch certain leaks and then create others—to fit nicely in the window.

The objective here is to design the window with purpose. To be very intentional—about your spending habits, yes, but also about what leaks you may be dealing with.

Again, it's not about patching every drop of water that may escape. It's about focusing on the leaks, understanding them, and being intentional about which ones you'll let in so the flowers in your life can grow.

Because we simply *have* to spend money in our lives. There's no situation where you can find that perfect pot, and no water seeps out.

Rather than trying to avoid spending money, you need to control the environment in which you spend—to steer those leaks in a certain direction, and to try to make the best of them.

By *managing* the leaks in your Spending Window™, you'll be in a much better position than you would be if you were to let your funds splash around haphazardly. And you will be in a much better position than you would be if you were to plug all the leaks in your spending—because you *can't* plug them all.

Similar to our food comparison, there's no solution where you just stop eating altogether. Our bodies need sustenance. And we can't just stop spending money. We need to cover our expenses, and if there's a little bit left over for our enjoyment, then so be it. We can plan accordingly. The truth is that we can decide which leaks we repair, which leaks we add, and which leaks we keep as they are.

Which Leaks Do You Plug? Which Leaks Do You Keep?

What if we reframe things and say there are no leaks in your Spending Window™?

What if there are only spigots in your window—spigots designed so you can water the plants of your life?

Those spigots may cost money, but they're intentional. They are a means to an end. And most importantly, you're aware of them all.

So, instead of seeing them in a negative light, like you might a leak, you can think of them as an investment in your future. You might see them as a way to gain control and awareness of your finances and improve your financial life.

As always, you must start by looking inward. To enhance anything in your life, you must first look at yourself. You've got to shift your focus back to you. Set an intention and ask yourself a series of guiding questions.

Which leaks do you plug?

Which leaks do you keep?

Will you adjust the size or scope of certain leaks?

Perhaps you sell your speedboat and buy a newer car. Maybe, now that the kids have flown the coop, you downsize so you can save more for retirement. Maybe you limit your dinners out to twice per week.

These are the types of leaks you must examine. And you need to remember that the goal here is simply to build healthier financial habits. Instead of beating yourself up because you can't cover all the leaks in your window, know that you can manage the leaks.

There's no being perfect. There's just no way. But there is such a thing as being in control. And in this scenario, you can make gaining financial control your end goal.

You see, if you control the way you spend your money, you can increase your happiness by a long shot. You can start to spend money on things you *want* to spend your money on, and you can increase your personal satisfaction—all while being mindful of your finances. Then you'll start to feel better. You'll likely feel more adequate, and definitely more self-sufficient.

Again, you'll be in control. And you'll stop beating yourself up over not having a solid handle on your budget.

Be in Control: On Saving for the Long Run
No matter how we frame it, being in control is useful.

Think of a married couple for a moment. Say Ahmed and Celia are both working—they're earning a generous combined income—yet every month they struggle to cover their expenses.

Now, that isn't to say Ahmed and Celia aren't saving for retirement. A little bit of money is taken from their paycheck automatically each month and put into their respective 401k accounts. The couple is saving for the long run; they feel that piece of their financial puzzle is working out just fine, which is great for them. Plus, they've automated their contributions.

But they have a cashflow problem. Ahmed and Celia create a Spending Window™ to help mitigate this, and another problem comes up. What happens is that they only focus on the leaks in their window. They pay close attention to *when* the money is leaving their wallet, or their bank accounts. And they discover they have a great deal of automated spending taking place.

Ahmed and Celia soon realize they need to take back control. They need to adjust those leaks! And so, the duo sits down for a candid discussion, and they agree to stop those automatic payments. They decide to start having their bills *mailed* instead.

This, they find, will allow them to talk more openly about their spending, experience their spending differently, and force them to identify the main sources of their financial challenges. It will also help them stay inside their Spending Window™.

And so, Ahmed and Celia begin to mindfully patch certain leaks in their financial pot. They fix the leaks that aren't serving them, which helps them:

1. **Improve their cash flow.**
2. **Build awareness of the outflow of their money.**
3. **Value their finances more.**

Another key benefit is that Ahmed and Celia make a habit of carefully considering what they choose to spend their money on. They build awareness of the leaks in their Spending Window™, and they develop a system where they can evaluate their expenses and decide whether they want to keep them in a clear and consistent way.

As a result of their window, Ahmed and Celia transform their lives, decrease stress, and improve their finances. You can do the same thing.

Cash Payments, Raises, and the Outflow of Your Money
Ahmed and Celia in our example above found that moving away from online bill payments, and instead requesting paper statements, helped them reexamine their finances.

This is because tangible payment methods—think check or cash payments rather than credit card payments—can actually activate the part of the brain linked to physical pain.[23] When we part with money, and the experience is physical (as it is when we fork over cash), we become more aware of the impact the expenditure may have on our lives and finances.

Another way to better manage the outflow of your cash? In behavioral finance, and in financial planning in general, one of the easiest ways to improve your financial situation is to increase your earnings. You might ask for a raise, or you might start to supplement your income.

The caveat here? More money, or more income, could help you solve your financial problems—to an extent. The problem is that it won't do much in the way of helping you manage the *outflow* of your money. That is, your spending.

You see, when it comes to keeping up with the Joneses, you need to ask yourself how much money you really need. Without a Spending Window™ in place, more money may

---

[23] et.apa.org/record/2008-12802-002

well lead to more spending, more extravagance, and more *problems*.

Now is the time to take back control. I urge you to do so by creating your Spending Window™. Another great thing about taking this important step is that you can build your window at any age.

It's Never Too Late to Create a Spending Window™
There are no excuses. It's not like certain people can't create a window because of their age or background or another factor. And while it may be easier to form new habits when you're younger, you *can* teach an old dog new tricks. It's just a bit more difficult to break those longer-term patterns.

This means that if you've been a frivolous spender your whole life, and now you're experiencing regret at the age of 80, it's going to be tough to readjust your mindset. It can happen, but it won't be easy the way it might be for a 20-year-old who has just begun to spend their own money.

There are many variables at play, though. And we know people have a difficult time with delayed gratification in this country. This can be hard to mitigate without a concrete plan—which, again, is where your window comes in. The Spending Window™ essentially forces delayed gratification. When you think about it, you're *forcing* that spending to happen at a later time, and so you inherently get that gratification.

A Spending Window™ will allow you to reap the benefits of financial mindfulness. If you don't see the results of your efforts right away, chances are you will down the road. Especially during your retirement.

Saving for Retirement: Compounding Returns and the Impact of Starting Early

There's a whole lot of impulsivity involved in spending—but it's never too late to save.

Let's use the example of saving for retirement. And let's start by discussing the dilemma of a recent college graduate.

Though most of us were recent college graduates at one point, it's more than likely that few of us remember what that period was like.

We were earning money—perhaps for the first time in our lives. We were deciding how much to put away, and how much to spend.

Many college graduates want to have fun now and save later. But is this a smart decision?

Allow me to introduce you to Mandy, a 24-year-old college graduate employed at a marketing firm. She earns $50,000 per year—an above-average salary for her age and experience—and lives alone in a mid-sized city. Mandy likes to see her friends outside the office; she doesn't care much to cook, and so she spends most of her disposable income on restaurants, bars, and entertainment.

If you haven't already guessed it, Mandy doesn't like to miss the party. She likes to make an appearance at every social event, and one of her guilty pleasures is to spend her hard-earned money on makeup and jewelry. She even has some debt on a credit card from visiting her favorite cosmetics shop a few too many times.

And so, at the end of each month, Mandy finds herself with barely enough cash to live. She's essentially living paycheck to paycheck, and she's always waiting for the next deposit to come in. The new grad knows she needs to cut back, but she's afraid she'll miss out on the best part of her life by doing so.

Retirement is over 40 years away—so what does it matter? It's not like Mandy doesn't contribute to her 401(k). She even gets a company match.

The truth is that Mandy might benefit from creating a Spending Window™. Impulsive spending isn't a great habit. Saving for the future is important, and while it doesn't need to be immediate, the benefits of starting early are expansive. In addition to building cash for major life purchases like marriage, a house, and student loan payments, saving from a young age can work wonders for your retirement.

Because if you're going to retire at the age of 62, you need to figure out how to get there financially. ***Say you plan to save roughly $200 per month, with an average return of 8%.***

The first thing to keep in mind is that the age at which you start to save will make a huge difference in your overall experience. The following table will provide further insights:

Retirement Funds Based on Age of First Savings

Think it doesn't matter when you start saving for retirement? Think again.

It's never too late, of course. But if you start saving for retirement at the age of 22, your account will look completely different than if you'd started saving at 32, or even 42.

*With all else equal—**by putting away $200 per month, with an average return of 8%**—the results may well astound you.*

Age You First Started Saving for Retirement	Retirement Savings at Age 62
22	$621,000
32	$272,000
42	$110,000

The difference is truly exponential. This is what Mandy from our example above might not have initially understood. Yet *that's* where the power of compounding interest comes in. Those early savings can lead to big results later on—because you're making interest on the interest you've earned, and those monetary sums tend to snowball over time.

Put simply, the sooner you build positive spending habits, the better. This is why I would argue that the sooner you start a Spending Window™, the better off you'll be financially. Like I've said, it's never too late—but aim to start young if you can. Rather than feeling overwhelmed by the idea of saving $200 each month, you can be more mindful of your spending habits *without* obsessing over every line item. The idea is to reexamine your saving habits on the spending side because that is what is generally the most fruitful.

So, when you can—when you're ready to make that commitment—go ahead and take that leap. I don't even want to call it a *leap*, because it's a lifestyle above all else, but nonetheless, I urge you to take the first step in your journey.

You'll learn to save more money by creating your Spending Window™, without being forced to work harder, and without having to rob Peter to pay Paul.

By building your own custom window, you'll simply learn to manage your spending. And you'll see compounding results over time.

A Word to Those Living Paycheck to Paycheck
It's relatively easy to continue along a saving path if you already have one in place. However, for most people in the United States, it's too difficult. In 2017, 78% of Americans disclosed living paycheck to paycheck.[24] That's a significant amount of people who weren't saving money!

Budgeting is all well and good—but it's challenging. No one wants to sit down and work out a budget. No one wants to go over each and every factor at play in their spending and impose limitations that are in many cases too hard to stick to. This is especially relevant for those who deal with a lot of uncertainty in their income and expenses.

I don't know if I'm going to make that much money this month, some might think.

I don't know when the next bill is going to come up.

---

[24] press.careerbuilder.com/2017-08-24-Living-Paycheck-to-Paycheck-is-a-Way-of-Life-for-Majority-of-U-S-Workers-According-to-New-CareerBuilder-Survey

And while budgeting may be difficult in the face of uncertainty, a Spending Window™ doesn't have to be. A window will eliminate much of the guesswork involved in managing your finances.

Do you think you don't have time to create a budget, or even develop a Spending Window™?

Well, think again. According to the Consumer Financial Protection Bureau, 20% of respondents shared that creating a budget was simply too much of a hassle.[25] But lots of things are a hassle. It can be a hassle to make time for the gym as well. It can be a hassle to eat right.

But we can still exercise, meal prep, and be mindful of the way we spend our money—even though some of us may see these things as a "hassle."

Saying that managing your finances is too much of a hassle is simply a cop-out.

There are simple solutions within reach. The first step is to create a Spending Window™.

After all, the hard-and-fast nature of time-restricted spending is much easier to follow than a budget. Why not make things simple, and build your window rather than relying on a spreadsheet full of numbers? If this isn't enough to convince you, I urge you to read the next section.

---

[25] files.consumerfinance.gov/f/documents/201702_cfpb_Consumer-Insights-on-Managing-Spending.pdf

Your Spending Window™ Is Your Ulysses Pact
Earlier we discussed "The Cracked Pot" parable.

Now we'll go over another analogy you can apply to your Spending Window™. This one involves what is known today as a Ulysses pact. In Homer's *Odyssey,* the protagonist Ulysses and his crew were sailing when they came upon the Sirens—a group of stunning women who sang songs so enchanting that the men who happened upon them would lose all control.

These men would stop acting rationally. They would be driven to madness. They would do anything to get closer to the Sirens and their subsequent death.

Now, Ulysses desperately wanted to experience the beauty of the Sirens. He also wanted to avoid falling victim to their spell.

So the witch Circe offered Ulysses a word of advice, suggesting that he plug his men's ears with wax, have them tie him to the mast of his ship, and ask that they release him only after they had sailed past the Sirens. That way Ulysses could experience their song without putting himself in peril.

So, Ulysses did just that. And while he listened to the Sirens, he begged and begged his crew to untie him—but they wouldn't let him loose. They couldn't hear him! That is, until a short time later, when they had passed the Sirens and removed the wax from their ears. Only then did they untie Ulysses.

And so, the hero was safe. The Sirens' magical song didn't lead to his demise.

Do you see the parallels here with intermittent spending? There's something to be said about having a plan outlined, carefully thinking it through, and making decisions that will serve you. For the best results, you should be making these decisions in a calm state of mind.

Because in stressful times, you might not be as rational as you'd like. And so, you need a framework in place that will help you navigate those challenging periods.

All it takes is a plan you can commit to: your Spending Window™.

Before We Move Forward
The truth is that you never know when the Sirens will start singing. You may feel compelled to cover the cost of happy hour drinks, an unexpected car repair, or a family emergency the second the expense comes up. But if you're tied to the mast of your ship, and your crew has wax in their ears, you'll be better equipped to stay on course.

So, make your Spending Window™ your Ulysses pact. Eliminate the distractions that arise when you're faced with a decision and adhere to the window you've set for yourself. It will make your life easier, and it may well improve your finances too.

This brings us to the topic of our next chapter: common pitfalls, and strategies for using your support system to overcome them.

Are you ready to talk about enlisting your family members to help monitor your intermittent spending, just as Ulysses enlisted his crew to survive the Sirens' call? With a little bit of help from your friends, you can gain control of your spending. This brings us to 10 common Spending Window™ pitfalls and some strategies for overcoming them. These strategies include the art of building a support network.

Chapter Seven
10 Common Pitfalls
And Strategies for Overcoming Them

We've discussed intermittent spending and what your Spending Window™ might look like. Now let's talk about some of the common traps you may fall into while going about this process.

From cheating to using cash without tracking that spending, we'll walk you through some of the mistakes far too many of us have made before. We'll also discuss the benefits of building a supportive team who can help you as you progress in your journey. With these insights, you can avoid the spending traps people face—or at least get back on track quickly.

With that, here are 10 pitfalls you'll want to avoid:

1. Cheating

Cheating is a common problem where intermittent spending is concerned. In many cases, people fall victim to impulse buys—say, an occasional cup of coffee—outside their Spending Window™.

But what does it mean to break your spending fast?

Often, what this looks like is that you're out with a friend or family member. You see something that you want to buy, and you simply go for it because it doesn't cost much. It isn't planned, and it isn't sneaky or malicious in any way, but it won't benefit you in the long term.

How can you mitigate this? One suggestion is to leave your credit card at home when possible. In the event of an emergency, try to use cash. Like we discussed in the last chapter, it's typically more difficult to part with cash because tangible payments activate the pain center in the brain.

Fight the urge to spend that money when you're out and about. Modify your use of credit card spending outside your window. Track your results and see how you can resist the urge to cheat.

2. Failing to Track the Cash You Spend

Cash isn't "free" money. There's no such thing. And so, you still need to track your cash payments.

Say you've set your window. Everything looks and feels right—but you are inadvertently playing the system. You are using cash around your window because you don't see it on your reports.

Cash is a double-edged sword in this way. And regardless of whether you let yourself spend cash outside your Spending Window™, you should track these expenditures. You also need to create a system where your spending truly makes sense.

Maybe you give yourself $20 per week for incidentals, and that's part of your Spending Window™. And maybe, outside your window, that's the maximum amount of cash you let yourself spend. Don't let it carry over from week to week—this isn't company vacation time we're talking about! Either spend it within a seven-day period, or refrain from spending it and allow the fund to reset the following week.

We talked about the importance of being in control, right? Tracking your cash spending will force you to be a little more thoughtful. Just keep that cash fund to a minimum. Avoid letting it turn into a seemingly endless slush fund you can use at your leisure outside your Spending Window™.

And again, be sure to keep track of all your cash spending. That way you'll know where every last cent of your money is going.

3. Relying on Automatic Payments

Automating your bill payments and online subscriptions can be a great thing—when you're aware of the payments you're making, that is.

We all need to hold ourselves accountable and take control of our spending. Automatic payments can be very helpful in some cases, but it's vital that you are aware of them all. Be sure to include the payments that occur less frequently, like auto insurance, which many of us pay once every six months.

Then, when you create your intermittent spending plan, make sure those payments fit inside your window.

How can you achieve this? Here's a tip: Either pause or stop each and every one of your automatic payments. Then, reconfigure the ones you want to keep inside your Spending Window™, so that you're mindful of where your money is going.

Say you're about to begin your own intermittent spending journey this week. You're in the process of establishing your window, and you're thinking about a car payment you plan to make on the first of the month for your Toyota RAV4.

The first thing you need to do is acknowledge the payment. Easy, right? And while you know the funds will be pulled from your account on the first of the month, you need to recognize that you might not know the exact time the payment will take place.

There is a chance the payment will fall outside your Spending Window™—but as long as you're aware of this, and you factor it in, and you truly understand your spending, then that's perfectly fine. I would only recommend this approach, though, for payments that are *necessary*.

It's fine if a car or mortgage or even an insurance payment is made outside your window, but things like gym payments and Netflix subscriptions shouldn't. I really want you to exert your control where you can if that makes sense.

And a great way to achieve this, in my experience, is to put an end to those payments and restart the ones you plan to continue making. I know this sounds ridiculous, but the truth is that it's a surefire strategy for figuring out which automatic payments you want to keep and which ones you want to cancel—no shortcuts.

4. **Prioritizing Credit Payments Over Debit Payments**

Nothing is *wrong* with using your credit card inside your Spending Window™. There's another common pitfall involved in this decision, though.

This pitfall involves a lack of awareness. And it applies to automatic payments or really any type of payment you make.

The idea is that with a debit payment, you see the funds coming out of your checking account. Often, credit card statements are nebulous—and you don't have access to them right away. You only see them every 30 days.

Debit payments, however, are shown coming out of your checking account the very day the payment takes place.

I will say, though, that there's a bit more protection with credit cards than there is with debit cards in the event of theft. Be cautious about this, but aside from that, I would absolutely recommend using a debit card as opposed to a credit card. It's a more tangible, immediate experience that will help you increase awareness of your spending habits.

5. Binge-Spending

Another common pitfall is binge-spending.

Going back to intermittent fasting, many people will overeat during their window—and the same thing applies to spending. The idea is that because your window is open, you can go to town and eat whatever you feel like eating. You may gobble down a couple of ice cream sundaes and skip the salad you planned to eat with dinner because you're inside your window, and you feel like overcompensating after hours of "good" behavior, and on paper that's okay.

Pro-Tip: Be weary of this. Try not to eat (or spend) more than you need. And while going overboard inside your window is certainly preferable to around-the-clock binge-eating, or constantly binge-spending, it's still important to be mindful.

In simple terms, you need to carefully consider the spending decisions you make—both inside and outside your window. Again, you need to be in control. And while your window can help facilitate that sense of control, you still need to practice mindfulness during those times you're allowed to spend.

Ultimately, the goal of a Spending Window™ isn't to give you a budget you need to abide by. It isn't to ensure you make intelligent financial decisions. Rather, the idea is to get in a better behavioral mindset and a more intentional thought process when it comes to your spending.

And just because you have a Spending Window™ in place, that doesn't mean you need to binge-spend. Financial literacy is an entirely different conversation, but it's still somewhat relevant here. You can visit the library instead of buying a stack of new books. You can purchase a used car in great condition instead of investing in a brand-new vehicle. You can be more intentional in your decision-making, avoid binge-spending when possible, and start small by practicing mindfulness.

Of course, you still need to set some money aside for extenuating circumstances—which brings us to the next item on our list here.

6. Failing to Set Up an Emergency Fund

We don't live in a vacuum. We can't anticipate every little thing that will affect us financially. We can, however, plan for emergencies and unforeseen circumstances. This means *you* can financially prepare for a wide range of situations that arise—without compromising the integrity of your Spending Window™.

This is where your emergency fund comes in. If you don't have one already, you should start one. You see, there may be times you'll need to spend some money outside your window—and that's perfectly fine. The key thing to define what constitutes an emergency and to determine how you'll spend money in these types of situations.

Going out for drinks with a friend, for instance, is not an emergency. Dipping into your fund to cover the cost of a cocktail or two would undeniably mean breaking your Ulysses pact.

The copay for your child's visit to urgent care, on the other hand? Now *that's* a valid emergency. Feel free to pull from your fund in this case. And be sure to track your spending throughout.

My main ask here is that you establish specific criteria to define what is an emergency from your perspective, and that you decide how you are going to cover the costs of these unforeseen events. The point here is to build awareness, and to start identifying when and how these unforeseen events happen so you can gain more control over your life and finances.

7. Making Your Window the Wrong Size or Shape

We're not perfect. We all make mistakes.

And that's just fine. It's totally normal. But when it comes to your Spending Window™, I want you to learn from the mistakes you make.

As you learn from them, you can adjust your window. You can reframe, or resize, your window for the best results.

Just as you don't want to allow yourself to spend for 23 hours of the day, you don't want to only give yourself 23 *minutes* of the day to spend your money. In this way, the size of your window is so important. You also need to

realize that it's fluid. You're not going to create your window and simply let it be for all of eternity.
Consider a real-life window for a moment. On cooler nights, you might enjoy the breeze. On hot days, when the AC is on—or when it's cold outside and you crank up the heat—you'll probably close your window.

Basically, you'll end up adjusting your window to the environment. The same thing applies to your Spending Window™. You can adjust it over time to gain more control over your life and finances. Going back to our example above, a 23-minute Spending Window™ may sound ridiculous. That isn't to say, though, that you shouldn't give yourself a 23-minute window just once or twice per week in order to challenge yourself.

Is it realistic in the long term? Maybe not. But why not try it out? See what happens and figure out what works for you. Your Spending Window™ isn't about what's right for everyone; it's about what's best for you and *your life*.

When you look at intermittent fasting, people appreciate patterns. They might want to commit to an 18-hour fast, or an every-other-day approach, or a one-meal-a-day system. These strategies are easy to remember. Where spending is concerned, it's going to be different. There are so many factors at play, and for this reason, you shouldn't be afraid to tailor your window to your needs. You can curate it based on the day or even the season. As a student, for instance, your Spending Window™ when you're away at college will probably look a little different from the window you adhere to when you're home on summer break.

It's okay if it varies. The important thing is that you have a concrete system in place.

8. Neglecting to Plan for Major Events

Need to buy a small gift for a birthday, anniversary, or another event?

Great. It should be relatively easy to make the purchase inside your Spending Window™.

Other major expenses are in many cases a different story. For example, you might not close on your first house inside your window because often, that decision is made for you. You can't just shift the timing of it.

What you can do is plan for the event. Will you be writing a check, or will you be making a wire transfer? One-time events, while difficult to schedule, really are the exception here. But you still need to be mindful.

I encourage you to conduct ample research when you make major purchases. Don't get carried away, and certainly don't spend more money than you were planning on spending. Keep in mind that one significant purchase, even if you adhere to your intermittent spending schedule, can destroy a year's worth of diligent saving.

If, for example, you are budgeting $15,000 for a new car, don't leave the dealership with a $20,000 vehicle. That one decision could destroy your budget. It's pretty critical that you keep this in mind because one step outside your Spending Window™ won't necessarily destroy your finances—at least not where your timing is concerned. A major purchase, though, can have dire consequences.

To mitigate these consequences, I urge you to plan for those bigger events. Aim to build empowering financial behaviors, and the benefits will follow.

9. Getting Overwhelmed

It's far too easy to be hypercritical of every purchase you make, or to feel anxious when you think about tracking all your expenses. If, after a couple of days with your window, you grow disheartened, you could bring in a professional—maybe a financial person who specializes in budgeting or debt management. This can help to lessen those feelings of despair and overwhelm. So please, don't be afraid to ask for help.

We've also talked about the importance of getting your friends, family, and coworkers involved in your intermittent spending journey. Sometimes, when you're feeling overwhelmed, talking things out can make a world of difference in lowering those stress levels and bringing you closer to the solution you've been waiting for.

The answer to your spending challenges may be obvious from the outside, and you're just not seeing it. A trusted friend or spouse or colleague can help take the emotions out of the process, helping you to reflect on your experience, modify your approach, and come out stronger.

It's all about course-correcting. To achieve this, you need a team of people by your side. You need to be malleable and resilient. And you need to remember that Rome wasn't built in a day, so to speak—and that anything in life that's worth something, you have to wait for.

With that, I invite you to be patient and celebrate those small successes. After a month or two, you may well notice some real changes. I'm confident you'll feel liberated by all the progress you make. Just recognize the results won't necessarily be immediate.

10. Falling Victim to Peer Pressure

We've touched on involving a small cohort of loved ones in your Spending Window™. We haven't yet discussed the dark side of those social situations.

Peer pressure is a very common intermittent spending pitfall. To avoid falling victim to peer pressure—to situations where your friends and family encourage you to spend outside your window—you need to create a window that accommodates your social life. As we discussed in our chapter on the novel coronavirus pandemic, social isolation can wreak havoc on our mental health, and I certainly don't want your personal relationships to suffer.

So if your Spending Window™ is so rigid that it doesn't allow you to socialize, I urge you to make changes. This doesn't mean you should overspend, but you should probably make adjustments as needed (and incorporate a healthy social life into your approach).

To this end, I think it's important that you involve your friends and family in this process. You can't keep your Spending Window™ a secret without a clear reason for doing so. Granted, you should steer clear of enablers, or people who seem to *want* you to spend money outside your window. If you notice these people are acting questionably, have a conversation with them—the same way you'd talk to a friend who keeps inviting you out for pizza while you're fasting.

After a while, these enablers may realize they need to back off some. And if they don't, then you can gently back away from them. Be proactive in removing yourself from situations where you're forced to break your own Spending Window™ rules.

Does this make sense? Good.

We've gone over 10 common pitfalls people face when building their Spending Window™, and some strategies for overcoming them. Now let's go over a handful of tips for success.

Tip #1 for Success: Build Your Support Network
One thing to keep in mind in your relationships is that you can't hold people's behavior against them if they don't know what your spending rules are. You have to be transparent and communicative about what you're doing.

This doesn't mean you need to tell every Tom, Dick, and Harry about your intermittent spending plan. This doesn't mean you should tell everyone in your circle about your newfound spending habits. The idea here is to inform the close friends and family who can best support you—and who can help you stick to your plan.

Of course, there are exceptions to the rule. Do you remember Kim and Joe from our Introduction? They actually decided not to tell anyone about their Spending Window™. The spouses believed that by working together, they could give each other the support they needed and hold each other accountable without any *need* for a third party. Their young kids had no spending capabilities, and they didn't want to worry them. And Joe, in particular, didn't want their social network to know they were struggling financially.

Ultimately, a support network can be beneficial, but it isn't the be-all, end-all of your experience. As an alternative to sharing your window with friends and family, you can turn to strangers on the internet for their support.

If you visit spendingwindow.com, you won't only find people who have completed their journey. You'll also find people who are *thinking* of embarking on their intermittent spending experience. There's really no one better to help you than all of us who have been there before.

Tip #2 for Success: Involve Your Spouse
I won't sugarcoat it: As you may well know, financial problems are among the leading causes of divorce here in the United States.[26] And by creating a Spending Window™ and *not* involving your spouse, I firmly believe you're looking for trouble.

You can learn so much from other people's experiences. This doesn't mean you should only turn to Spending Window™ veterans for advice and support. You should also rely on—and even involve—your spouse in your intermittent spending experience.

First, I think it's important to reassure your spouse that they don't have to adhere to your window as well, although they may want to do so. (They may also decide to develop their own Spending Window™ around their unique needs.) In any case, your spouse must be aware and supportive of your window.

Who knows? Your partner may even have some great insights into your spending habits that you can keep in mind while you craft your window. That, along with your spouse's unending support, will set you up for success.

---

[26] psychologytoday.com/us/blog/insight-is-2020/201212/how-financial-problems-stress-cause-divorce

Remember that by adhering to your window, you *and* your family will benefit. You're a team, and you all have skin in the game here. With this in mind, you can work together toward success.

Tip #3 for Success: Hold Each Other Accountable
Hey guys, I just created a Spending Window™. Here's what it is: XYZ.

If you see me spending money during this time, I'd appreciate it if you could just help me out and give me a gentle reminder. Maybe avoiding asking me to go out on a Thursday night, because that's outside my window and I don't want to be tempted.

This is a very legitimate conversation to have with the people in your circle. Your friends will respect you more for communicating with them. And together, you can hold each other accountable.

Sometimes, holding each other accountable means challenging each other. I have a couple that tried this once: David and Margaret.

Now, Margaret liked to kayak in her free time, and David liked to stay home and watch movies. Despite their differences, the two of them created a compelling challenge that combined these hobbies with their respective Spending Windows™.

Here's how the challenge worked: If either spouse caught the other stepping outside their window the offender would have to put some money in a pool that would fund the other person's activity. So, if David caught Margaret spending money outside her window, Margaret would have to give her husband cash for a movie or maybe a nice dinner at home. And if Margaret saw David spending money outside his window, she would receive a bit of money for kayaking—or maybe they'd go on a nice hike together, even though David wasn't very outdoorsy.

If anything, this challenge reveals that you can have fun while holding each other accountable. This brings to mind another couple. Jared and Lori were planning their son's bar mitzvah when they too decided to challenge themselves. They said, "If we can keep our spending under a certain amount, we'll reward ourselves after the event."

They decided to create a Spending Window™ in order to achieve their goals. Events like bar mitzvahs and weddings, as you may well know, can get out of hand financially—but the hosts made a commitment. Jared and Lori challenged themselves as a unit to limit their spending.

Their son's celebration turned out great. The best part was they didn't have to cut any corners. And afterward, Jared and Lori were able to go out and do something fun, just the two of them.

This reinforces that we really have to hold each other accountable. It's like participating in a weight loss challenge with a friend or two—you have to say it out loud, share your goals, and only then will you be in a position to work toward achieving them.

It's natural to want to keep things to yourself. Maybe you're embarrassed. Maybe you don't want to admit that you're dealing with some spending-related challenges. It's like admitting you're an alcoholic—no one *wants* to say it. But finding a group of likeminded people, or at the very least telling others, is arguably the best thing you can do.

Then, and only then, can others help you. They might even want to get involved too.

"Let's do it together," they might say. "Let's work to hold each other accountable."

How would that make you feel? There are many pitfalls you may experience along your journey, but the truth is that a network of supportive people can help you get back on track quickly. This will be very useful as you move forward in your journey.

Guess what? That journey starts now.

Conclusion
Progress Over Perfection

Thank you for sticking with me over the course of this book. I hope you've found the content valuable. I certainly appreciate the benefits a thoughtfully crafted Spending Window™ can bring, and I know many of my clients do too. Done mindfully, intermittent spending can be a remarkable process with monumental results.

And now *you* have everything you need to get started. Together we've gone over dozens of tools that will help you design the perfect window for your unique set of circumstances. We've outlined a wealth of strategies for success in your arsenal, along with some common pitfalls you'll want to avoid—or at least, address—along the way.

Before I let you go, I'd like to take a moment to revisit the couple from our Introduction.

Do you remember Kim and Joe? The couple lived in a New York City suburb and struggled to build their savings account. Though their financial situation wasn't *dire*, they just couldn't seem to grow their money beyond what they needed for basic cash flow. And so, they set their terms, committed to a 16:8 spending window, and decided to take it month by month. Their goal was to grow their savings from $0 to $25,000 within one year.

Now, a year hasn't gone by just yet. And while the spouses' experience hasn't been entirely free from bumps in the road, they've already made great progress as a result of intermittent spending. In fact, they're closer than ever to reaching their goal.

Their first month in, Kim and Joe increased their savings to $700. This wasn't enough to reach $25,000 in one year, but it was solid progress, nonetheless. Perhaps most importantly, the spouses made crucial behavioral changes. They became more mindful of their expenditures, and they pledged to make continued progress and compound their savings.

Two months in, Kim and Joe grew their savings account to $1,800. Talk about a snowball effect! They also experimented and tried a no-spend weekend at one point. It worked well enough, although they were concerned the kids would be bored. They also struggled with food during this time, since they had a family day at the beach and their eight-year-old wanted a snack.

But Kim and Joe pushed through. Yes, they slipped up from time to time. Once they used cash for morning coffees outside their window. One Sunday morning, Kim used cash to tithe at church outside her window. Joe needed to fill his gas tank before work one day. Cell phone bills they'd forgotten about popped up outside their Spending Window™, and Kim and Joe paid them to avoid incurring a late fee.

There were other challenges too: Kim and Joe still spent money on lunches during the week, although eventually they had a discussion about pricing and decided instead to pack meals from home. Joe had an urgent visit to Home Depot one Saturday morning outside their window. Additionally, he and Kim went out to eat one Friday night, lost track of time, and had to pay their bill at 9 p.m.—an hour outside their window. Kim also had a tough time navigating her weekly girls' night expenses. She consulted Joe and decided to add another $100 to their cash allowance and give the funds to a friend at the beginning of the evening to avoid spending money after her 8 p.m. cutoff.

Both Kim and Joe grew annoyed at the restrictions they'd imposed at the end of their first month—they felt limited. Some of their slip-ups seemed unavoidable, and they worried they weren't truly living. The process of finding leaks in their proverbial financial bucket, however, forced a conversation. It revealed to Kim and Joe that they could be more mindful of their spending without overdoing it. Eventually, they changed their window to be more stringent on weekends and less stringent on weekdays. They were pleased with the changes and decided to continue making incremental changes over time.

Some other changes they made: Kim and Joe eliminated a few subscriptions they didn't really use. (Were Netflix *and* Hulu really necessary?) They adjusted their dining out plans to be less frequent but more meaningful, and they started visiting a nice restaurant one night per week instead of ordering in anytime they felt like it.

They began saving money, a little bit at a time. And now Kim and Joe are making their way closer and closer to that $25,000 annual savings goal. As a direct result of their Spending Window™, Kim and Joe have completely transformed their financial lives. They're on track to have real savings. They're no longer worried about their family's future. They're living proof that when it comes to intermittent spending (and many other areas of our lives), progress is far better than perfection.

I'm very happy for Kim and Joe, and I hope you are too—which brings me to an important question: Are you ready to get started on *your* intermittent spending journey?

Learn more, choose your window, and see how others are doing:

www.spendingwindow.com

www.facebook.com/SpendingWindow

www.ingramcontent.com/pod-product-compliance
Lightning Source LLC
Chambersburg PA
CBHW060852220526
45466CB00003B/1345